BIRTHDAY SUIT

TO KIAN :)

TYLER DURMAN

EIGHT TOE BOOKS

EIGHT TOE
BOOKS

Birthday Suit
Eight Toe Books / March 2012

Published by Eight Toe Books
Laguna Beach, California

Cover Design by Devin Dailey
Book Design by Jeremy Inman and Todd Ford

Printed in La Vergne, Tennessee, in the United States of America

February 2012 ISBN 978-1-4675-1803-1
Eight Toe Books and Birthday Suit are the trademarks or registered trademarks of Tyler Durman Inc.

To Spencer Bement.

If there is any beauty in the telling of these stories, it is because of all that you've taught me about writing. I am forever your apprentice.

Stories

Naked 1

Nuns 17

Rodney 31

Running 55

On Slanted Hill 73

The Hero and the Target 85

Chew'n and Spit'n 93

Frogs 99

Out of the Fog 119

Africa 131

For Kristen

Naked

I'd been in the same chair for the best part of two days, and now sat alone, staring at the doorknob. My butt ached but I hesitated to rub it, for fear the psychologist might catch me and think I had issues.

The small room had followed my example and fallen silent, as if waiting with me. The only movement I could sense was the twirling of excitement in my stomach.

A wooden table sat to my back, pressed into the corner of the chalk colored walls, and reflecting the florescent bulb overhead. The only color in the space rose from the plush carpet, which, as far I could tell, was either green or brown.

After filling in hundreds of little dots with a #2 pencil, I had slipped out, handed my papers to a secretary, washed my hands and reentered the room. The paper towel I had used to turn the knob sat behind me, precisely folded and placed at parallels to the front corner of the table.

I was twenty-two, and the psychologist, a trained "career expert," would be turning that knob any second to give me the answer I'd been searching for most of my life.

As I waited, I smiled. My mind flashing back half a lifetime to the hours I'd spent preparing for my future while standing shirtless on my brother's bed.

*   *   *

I was eleven, it was 1969, and though my chest had no hair and my voice was high, I was pretty sure I was going to be an internationally famous rock star. While my brother was wasting time with girls, I was sneaking into his room to sing along with his Beatles records.

I reminded myself of Paul.

I'd heard John was dating Yoko and knew this had trouble written all over it. They'd need a replacement, which I figured was a good thing for me.

Sure I was young, but two other kids my age were doing pretty well, and I thought if Michael Jackson – a Jehovah's Witness, and Donny Osmond – a Mormon, could be famous, why not me? I went to Sunday school.

All I needed was my big break.

It came when I was fourteen, and my six chest hairs

were proof I was ready. They were perfectly balanced, three per side.

The church was having a Christmas banquet, and they asked me to sing a solo. They'd requested a carol about decking the halls with Holly's bowels, and though I didn't understand the words, I came prepared to rock.

I was the headliner so everyone had to be patient while the guest speaker rambled on about his adventures. He'd been flying little planes into darkest Africa and landing on perilous strips in the jungle so he could get doctors in to save lives.

Blah. Blah. Big deal.

But then when he was finished, the place went crazy with applause, which I took as a good sign.

I grabbed the microphone, held it between both palms, nodded to my sister to start the background cassette, put my left foot out in front, and sang like a blackbird in the dead of night. I arched my back on all the important notes and strained my face to show my passion.

As I hit the last line I raised one hand into the air, fingers spread, just like I'd practiced on my brother's bed. At my final fa-la-la, I closed my eyes, abruptly pulled my hand into my chest with a fist, rocked my head back and bowed.

I was amazing!

Then, silence.

I opened one eye. My mom and sister began to clap, a few old ladies joined in, and I knew this wasn't the demographic I was after.

The emcee said, "Well that was" - pause - "pleasant" and the audience looked around the ceiling as if searching for spiders. In that instant I knew my calling was to be a pilot.

I never told anyone, but on the way home I felt relieved I wasn't going to be a rock star because famous singers have to shake a lot of hands. I'd always had a problem touching people's hands, and though I knew it wasn't normal, shaking caused me anxiety and the uncontrollable urge to wash.

There were a lot of things like this I kept secret.

Once, when I was a teenager, I found myself alone inside a public bathroom standing in front of the exit in a mock walking position. The room had air dryers so I couldn't use a paper towel to open the door, toilet paper was too thin, and the thought of using my shirt made me feel nauseous. My anxiety was so consuming that it seemed to leak from its place in my chest and fill the tile-covered room.

The air felt dirty and I was drowning in it.

I waited in that position for about fifteen minutes until someone pushed the door from the outside. As they came in, I pretended I'd just been about to open the door myself, and slipped past without having to touch the handle. I could breathe again.

I felt ashamed about all this because I couldn't control it, so I got pretty good at hiding things. No one had ever caught me standing with my head against the back door after my parents went to sleep, trying to stop myself from checking the lock again, even though I'd already checked it nine times. No one knew that I felt compelled to count stairs and to always start climbing with my right foot. And no one understood that my need to line objects up in perfect parallels came from such an unhealthy place.

People didn't talk about Obsessive Compulsive Disorder, so I spent a lot of energy pretending to be normal.

I thought I was the only one.

This pilot-in-Africa-thing seemed great because I'd be alone most of the time, and even if someone figured out how weird I was, who was going to make fun of me over there? What, was a baboon going to laugh at me? If one did, I'd make a comment about his funny colored butt and we'd be even.

Flying into jungles excited me, so at eighteen I went to the same college that the pilot from the Christmas banquet had attended, and two years into it, signed up for flight school.

Things were looking up. I was twenty, had at least twelve chest hairs, and a plan for my future.

To get into flight school I had to take an eye exam, and

because I couldn't see the numbers hidden in the colored circles, they told me I couldn't fly.

"Colorblind people can't see the color coded lights on runways," they said. When I said I didn't mind, they suggested that I'd end up crashing into other planes, which is frowned on around airports.

This seemed picky and I was sad until I decided to become a professional soccer player. I was doing pretty well on the college team so it felt like a great fit.

By this time I'd learned that it's good to have a backup plan, so I figured if soccer didn't work out, I'd just move to California and become a professional surfer. But then in my last year of college I got gout, which eventually led to the amputation of two toes. And although my feet were still perfectly balanced, four-per-side, this meant that even my backup plan was out.

No one ever got famous hanging eight.

My grades were average, but I'd always suspected I was just a misunderstood genius, so for a brief time at the end of college I considered becoming a surgeon. People around school would say, "Wow, Dr. Durman huh?" and girls thought I was cool.

But then it dawned on me that if I couldn't touch a door handle, cutting open sick guys and sticking my hands inside was probably not a wise career move.

And that was it. I was out of ideas.

*   *   *

So here I was, twenty-two, and sitting in a small pale room staring at a doorknob. There had to be something a colorblind-eight-toed-secret-OCD-sufferer was good for.

Maybe my tests would show that I was best suited to be a feature film star. Yeah, I liked that because I could live a reclusive life in Europe between movies, and have a stunt double touch things for me. I wouldn't have to hide my weirdness anymore because everyone would just think I was an eccentric artist.

The doorknob turned and the professional walked in.

I slipped my hands into my pockets.

She sat on the table and smiled.

I smiled back.

Here it comes.

"Sorry to keep you."

"That's okay."

"We had to run the results twice because we thought there was a mistake."

I held my breath. Maybe they'd figured out how abnormal I was.

"After a second review, there was no mistake. We've just never seen anything this extreme before."

I didn't know what to say so I looked at one of her shoes. She had small feet.

"It seems that the job you're best suited for is to be a forest ranger."

I looked up. "A forest ranger?"

"A forest ranger."

"Okay. But how come?"

"There's evidence that you may be the most extreme introvert we've tested in seventeen years of doing this, and I suppose as a forest ranger you'd be out in the woods for months without seeing another human being."

Hmm. This sounded good.

But then I was confused.

"Um, but I like most people."

"Yes, it's a common misunderstanding that introverts are always shy or don't like people. What it means is just that you are emotionally and psychologically drained by being around others, while extroverts are energized by others."

"Huh." I nodded as if Freud and I had just been discussing this very thing over wiener schnitzels that morning.

She tilted her head to the side the way some people do when they're feeling sorry for someone. "Can I give you some advice?"

"Sure."

"No matter what you end up doing, make sure you get a lot of time to yourself. If you don't, you'll experience mental and emotional exhaustion that could lead to burnout. You have to accept that it's okay to be who you are."

I wondered if she could save money buying children's shoes.

"Tyler?"

I realized I should say something. "Is there any way to fix this?"

She laughed. "It doesn't mean there's something wrong with you, just that you're different than most people."

"A forest ranger huh?"

"Yup. Or some other job like it."

I thanked her and when I stood to go she said, "Just so you know, your OCD is going to complicate all this."

Yikes! She knew. I just nodded slowly.

"You need to be careful not to become a total recluse and shut out the world. Even extreme introverts need people."

She handed me a business card, and though I didn't want to touch it, I took it with the tips of my finger and thumb. She said that if I ever needed to talk, this person would be good.

I figured there must be something really wrong with me for her to suggest this, so I just sort of nodded again and hugged her to avoid shaking her hand. "Well thanks for everything, and maybe I'll see you in the woods one day."

I felt stupid for saying this.

I took a step toward the door and froze. She was kind, so she reached around me and turned the doorknob and smiled. Her hands were tiny and I almost said something about children's mittens, but instead headed for the parking lot wondering what kind of car a forest ranger should drive.

A Land Cruiser with big tires sounded cool.

So the next month I took a job as a high school teacher, which after some ups and downs led to a career as a speaker who travels on crowded airplanes all the time and tells stories to over a quarter million people a year and has to shake many of their hands and now lives in Los Angeles where there are 2.5 people per square foot.

I've discovered that she was right. I do need a lot of alone time.

*　　　*　　　*

The people who were closest to me always noticed my hand thing and assumed I was afraid of germs. As time slipped past I just played it off as a joke and they never knew it was only one leaf on my OCD tree. I was too embarrassed to tell anyone how much my struggles consumed my daily thoughts and energy.

My obsessions and compulsions kept me on the slippery edge of an abyss. They wanted to pull me into a dark place where I would no longer be able to function in the real world.

I needed something to hold on to, to protect me from falling in, so I made a rule that I'd always choose people over my struggles. Like if someone reached out to shake, I promised myself I'd put my palm in theirs, even though I knew I'd feel intense anxiety and obsess about my hand until I could wash it.

Like a rope, this rule gave me something to cling to so I wouldn't fall into the full control of my OCD. It drained a lot of energy, but I didn't want to end up like those people who can't leave their house. I still hold onto this same rope today.

When I became a dad I was relieved that my anxiety never kicked in when I touched or was touched by either of my sons. And yet as they grew, I continued to hide the depth of my struggles even from them.

*   *   *

As my career expanded, I decided to find a quiet place to live, so I moved to the Island of Kauai. I bought a little plantation cottage that sat at the end of a long drive and was surrounded by fields with nothing but horses. I felt so lucky because the property was serene and beautiful, and looked like the cover of a book I'd want to read.

It was private enough that unless someone came down the driveway, they would never know it was there. This seclusion helped me when I returned from a speaking tour, and my little home became my retreat and safe haven.

But soon things began to change.

One of the beautiful things about Hawaiian culture is the notion of "Ohana," which means "family." They value everyone as a brother, sister, uncle or auntie. And while I love this notion, it created a problem as I began to make friends.

Pop-bys.

Lots of nice people began stopping by for unexpected visits.

"Aloha, we were just in the area," they'd say, as they shook my hand and sat on my lanai to talk story. While I thought they were kind to visit me, my smile hid my exhaustion.

I couldn't ask them to stay away, so because of my sensitivity to the culture, I arrived at a solution.

Nudity.

24/7 I just stopped wearing any clothes whatsoever when I was home.

While I think that most males will go to extraordinary lengths to catch a glimpse of a naked woman, few people ever want to see a naked man. Especially a white guy in his fifties who spends lots of time bent over working in the yard wearing nothing but gardening gloves.

Innocent people would pop-by only to discover me nude and waving to them from my ride-on lawn mower. One couple pulled in to find me bent into the open hood of my Land Cruiser with nothing but an oily rag slung over my shoulder.

As it turned out, seeing a naked old guy has the same affect on people that rat poison has on rodents. After exposure, you just sort of limp away and hope to find a dark place to die.

The pop-bys dropped off almost immediately, and things were looking up. I did feel guilty about the psychological scars I was causing, but I just couldn't think of any other solutions. And besides, I rarely had to do laundry.

People were still nice when they'd see me at the grocery store or fish market, and the only ones who saw me naked after this were the horses.

With my peaceful life secure again, I could breathe. But as time went by I became more of a recluse. My friends pointed this out but I dismissed it. I would travel and tell stories about how to love well, come home exhausted and spend days, or even weeks, completely alone.

The longer I did this, the more my OCD rose to the surface of my days. It started to consume all my energy and attention. I knew this was dangerous and longed to feel close to someone, but couldn't bring myself to tell anyone the truth.

Pretending was exhausting. And so was the isolation it caused.

I felt an affinity with Eleanor Rigby, and all the other lonely people.

One day, after a couple of weeks of not leaving my property, the things that my "career expert" had said all those years earlier, came to mind. I was rinsing off in my outdoor shower, and it dawned on me that I had fallen into the very things she had warned me to avoid.

I had become reclusive and was walking my journey alone. This was the case even when I was around people, because none of them knew the whole truth about me.

The irony hit hard; I had created a lonely life because I was afraid of rejection.

When I closed my eyes to rinse the shampoo, I made myself a significant promise. I decided that one day I'd let someone see the naked truth about me. And even though I could feel my hands shaking against my scalp at the thought, I felt something like hope fill my chest. Maybe this meant that I wouldn't always have to bear my secret alone.

I turned off the water, stood there dripping wet, and realized I had never thanked the psychologist for reaching

around me that day, and opening the door. I wanted something nice for her, so I decided that I'd send gift card to Macy's. I'd heard they were having a s kid's shoes.

I smiled, knowing this would make her hap reached for my towel. As I did, I noticed a standing beyond the fence just staring at me. I as was because he was jealous.

around me that day, and opening the door. I wanted to do something nice for her, so I decided that I'd send her a gift card to Macy's. I'd heard they were having a sale on kid's shoes.

I smiled, knowing this would make her happy and reached for my towel. As I did, I noticed a gelding standing beyond the fence just staring at me. I assumed it was because he was jealous.

Nuns

When I was nine, I had a crush on a nun. Her name was Maria.

I saw her in a movie called *The Sound of Music* and told my brother I was going to marry her. He told me I was dumb because she was dating Jesus, which didn't seem fair to me. I didn't even know Jesus was allowed to date, and how was I supposed to compete with him?

I drifted to sleep that night singing, "How do you solve a problem like Maria? How do you steal her from the Son of God?"

When I woke I wondered if she'd seen that trick where you make your dog play dead and then raise him back to life, thinking that a miracle might impress her. But then I heard that Jesus had raised an actual dead guy from the grave, and I knew I was screwed.

My brother told me later that all the nuns were dating Jesus, and this really messed with my head. It had a profound affect on my early ideas of God.

And of nuns.

But then I grew up and was able to sort out all the confusion.

Over time I had the chance to meet some actual nuns, and several of them became my friends. Their love for people is beautiful to me, and I've been surprised to discover how much fun they are.

*   *   *

My favorite of these friends, Sister Catherine, called and asked if I'd come and speak at the large high school for girls that she runs. I'd been there before, and she wanted to know if I'd come back and focus on the subjects of "dating, romance and sex."

As she asked, I interrupted and said, "I'm sorry Sister, but what were the topics?"

"Dating, romance and sex," she repeated.

I said, "Forgive me, but my cell just dropped out for a second there. You said 'dating, romance and what?'"

"And sex," she said a bit louder.

I sighed, "You'll never believe it but someone just sneezed. Can you repeat that?"

"SEX!" She almost shouted it.

Then a giggle danced across her tongue and I knew she'd figured out that I was just trying to see how many times I could get a nun to say the word sex.

She laughed, "I know what you're doing Tyler, and I'm not going to say it again."

I said, "Four times makes me very happy thank you."

"You're a bad man."

"I know I am Sister."

We both laughed and went on to plan the day.

Sister Catherine is just five feet tall and embodies the full joy of God's love.

The day arrived and it was quite an experience to speak about those topics with about thirty nuns decked out in their Habits and beads sitting all in a row against the back wall.

I felt like God was watching me.

I'd promised the girls that at the end of our time together, I'd answer any questions they had. I told them that no question was off limits, that there was a box they could use with anonymity for that purpose, and that I'd randomly pull their questions and do my best with them.

I finished my final keynote and asked for the box. As I reached inside I said, "And here's the first one."

Because I wanted to honor my promise to answer any question, I read it aloud without first reading it to myself.

This plan was flawed.

"How come boys like big boobs better than small boobs?"

The girls giggled, and I tried not to look at anyone in particular, for fear they'd think I was searching for an example. I became acutely aware that I was the only male in the room, and at the exact same time every nun across the back leaned forward in her chair and tilted her head just slightly to the side.

Their motion was so precise and synchronized that it seemed like they'd practiced it together in nun school. They were the Religious Rockettes.

I took a breath and it felt like God had just shushed all the angels and leaned over the balcony of Heaven to see what I'd say.

I fumbled mentally because I was trying to remember how Maria was built in that movie, thinking this might be a good place to start.

Sometimes I am very dumb.

My next thought was to mention that Jesus dated all the nuns, which meant this question made a wrong assumption.

I whispered a silent prayer and God told me this was not a very good answer because Jesus didn't really date nuns.

I was grateful for His help.

I looked at Sister Catherine in the back row and she smiled and nodded.

I knew I needed to tell the truth.

"Well, I can't speak for all boys," I said, "I can only speak for myself."

The row of nuns leaned still further forward.

"I've dated women with different kinds of bodies, and all I can tell you is that the sexiest person I've ever dated had very small..."

And then my brain unraveled. It froze. I couldn't think. Inside my head, nothing but empty space. I tried to form an idea, find a word, but the silence and all those eyes in the room paralyzed me. And then all at once a thousand thoughts flooded in, but they were all tangled.

As this was happening, the words I'd just said seemed to swing over the crowd like a church bell, resounding again and again "... the sexiest person I've ever dated had very small..." – "... the sexiest person I've ever dated had very small..." – and so on.

It would have been difficult to see, but I shook my head just slightly to attempt to jar any word loose that would make sense. I didn't know if it was okay to say boobs, even though it was in the question. Then it struck me that I'd just said "sexiest" as though there was some sexy scale in my mind or something, which there is, but this went against all the ideals I'd spoken about all day.

I had to complete my sentence so I decided to just use the normal anatomical descriptive word, but couldn't find it in my brain anywhere. I could think of lots of other words that are used around town for this body part, but the word "breasts" eluded me.

I gulped and the word jumped into my mind, so I blurted it out louder than I should have.

"Breasts!"

Pause.

Silence.

Everyone stared at me.

My next words came quickly as I tried to distract everyone from what I'd just exclaimed with fervor.

"So-I'm-not-sure-it's-true-that-all-boys-feel-that-way-about-the-size-of-um-well-you-know-um-so-let's-look-at-another-question-shall-we?"

I nodded to myself and reached back into the box.

Later, on the airplane I thought of all the great answers I could have given. The ones that have to do with a woman's real value and that her visual appeal has more to do with how she carries and feels about herself than her shape, and that true beauty comes from inside, and how temporary physical beauty is anyway, and all that.

But none of this had come to my mind on the spot.

Sometimes I wish I were smarter.

All of this made me miss Maria.

She would have known what to say, or even what to sing. She seemed to enjoy breaking into spontaneous song at precisely the right moment, but the only song that came to my mind was, "These are a few of my favorite things," which would have been inappropriate, given the question at hand.

To my relief, the rest of the questions were easy.

After the Q&A, everyone applauded and I was happy that in a matter of minutes I'd be out of this sea of estrogen. I was afraid that Sister Catherine was going to be mad at me, so I headed for the opposite side of the room. My plan was to stay long enough to be polite, and then make my escape.

I chatted for a few minutes with some of the students and nuns, and just as I was about to leave, a twelfth grade girl named Keiko came over and asked if she could get some advice. She was wondering if she was handling a situation the right way.

I said I'd help if I could, and we found a couple of folding chairs.

She explained that she'd been dating a boy for five months, and that her parents had just told her they only wanted her seeing boys who were both Japanese and Roman Catholic, of which he was neither.

I asked how she had responded, and she said that she'd told them she would honor their wishes until she was eighteen, and asked if at that time they'd be open to getting to know him and his family a bit better, so they could reopen the discussion. They had agreed.

I smiled and told her that I thought she'd done the right thing. I explained that she'd not only respected her boyfriend and parents, but that she'd also respected herself.

With a relieved smile she said, "You really think so?"

"Absolutely. In fact you ought to write a book for girls. The way you're handling this thing shows tons of wisdom."

She thanked me, even though I'd done very little, and stood to go. As she did I said, "I'm proud of you Keiko."

When the words crossed the space between us, she collapsed back into her metal chair with such sudden force that everyone in the room looked our way. It was as if the muscles in her legs had failed. As she landed, she burst into tears.

I froze in my seat. I had no idea what had just happened.

Everyone in the room had stopped talking and was staring at us. I was afraid Sister Catherine was going to come over and hit me with a Bible or something.

Keiko's tears were gushing.

All I could figure was that she must have misunderstood what I'd said; so I said it again, only this time slower and louder.

"I'm proud of you."

This seemed to make her cry harder, which confused me.

Sometimes males don't understand females. I know this because I have a girlfriend.

I sat there feeling helpless and decided to keep my mouth shut, which I've learned is often a good thing to do in the presence of a crying female.

As I waited, she calmed herself and said, "I'm sorry."

She was wiping her face and I was still afraid to talk because I didn't want to say something stupid. I'd spent a lot of money on my master's degree but had nothing relevant in my head.

I should have studied harder.

She took a deep breath, wiped her face again, settled her shoulders, and looked me in the eyes.

"My mom and dad have never said they're proud of me. Not even once."

She said it quietly, as if telling herself a secret.

Her tears swelled again.

"Never?"

"Never."

Some of us spend our lives healing from the hurts of our childhood.

"I'm sorry Keiko."

"Nothing I ever do is enough for them." Her head shook slightly. Her eyes were full of longing.

"Well I'm proud of you. I really am. If I had a daughter, I'd want her to be just like you."

She could tell I meant this, blinked new tears and said, "Thank you. I'll never forget that you said that to me."

I think it's hard to be a girl these days, and that the rest of us can make their journey a lot easier.

We talked for a few more minutes, and then as she walked away, a lot of emotions were left floating in her wake. I don't know how long I stood there, but a touch on my arm jerked me from my thoughts.

It was Sister Catherine. She'd snuck up and put her hand on my elbow. I think her Habit was some kind of cloak of silence or something.

I looked down at her, and my heart skipped a beat because I'd never been yelled at by a nun before. Weird, but right then I wondered what someone could possibly give a nun for her birthday.

Sneakers? Do they ever jog or play tennis? Do nuns even have feet?

She raised her pointer finger and signaled me to lean down. I inhaled and bent to listen to what she wanted to speak into my ear.

"Tyler."

It was just a whisper.

"Yes."

"You handled that boob question quite well." She patted my arm and smiled.

Phew! It was nice to know God wasn't mad at me.

"And I heard what you said to Keiko, and I'm proud of you!"

I didn't know if it was okay to hug a nun or not, but I gave her a big one anyway, my face pressed against the side of her vale and cheek. She smelled very clean.

She hugged me back and as she did, I realized that I had needed to hear those words as much as Keiko had.

I suppose we all do.

We let go and she grabbed my arms, looked up and said, "If I had a son, and I'm pretty sure I never will, I'd want him to be just like you." And her words caught in my throat.

I nodded a moist eyed thank you.

*　　　*　　　*

Later, sitting on my plane, I realized that I'd developed a little crush on Sister Catherine. I figured this was okay because Maria never calls.

*　　　*　　　*

Sister Catherine, I know you're reading this somewhere, and I just want to say that I think Jesus is pretty lucky to be dating you.

Rodney

In the thriller *The Fly*, a brilliant scientist attempts to teleport himself, but his molecules become blended with those of a housefly that found its way into the telepod. It doesn't take him long to discover that girls aren't very attracted to hybrid fly-men, and his life and body begin to unravel. It doesn't end well.

Now picture a lanky nine-year-old boy climbing into that telepod. Only instead of a fly, there's a beaver, a squirrel and a ferret. What you'd end up with is Rodney, the kid assigned to be my little brother for the ten weeks of my summer vacation in Florida.

Two hours a week, on Tuesdays. Just me and rodent-boy.

He was one lucky kid because I was twenty-one, fresh out of college and excited to impart my vast wisdom.

We were introduced at a community center, where

the air conditioning was set too cold and the walls were painted too white. As he walked toward me, it seemed his steps were temporary attempts to stop the weight of his front teeth from causing him to fall forward.

His little hands worried against one another while his head darted this way and that, like a small mammal scanning a field for predators.

Squirrels groom themselves. Rodney did not. His smell got to me before he did. His greasy hair stuck to his shiny forehead, and his crumpled clothes hung loosely from his narrow shoulders, with stains all down the front.

He looked like he lunched in a dumpster.

One advantage any beaver would have over Rodney is that its enormous incisors point down and are useful for cutting wood. Rodney's pointed strait out and were only useful for embarrassment. I reluctantly extended my hand beneath their shadow, while secreting my other into a pocket to reach for my Purell.

When his damp hand shook mine, he looked at his own feet, as if eye contact would overwhelm him. I imagined that the mean kids at school must have a heyday with him. He'd be an easy target on any playground.

When he spoke, it was slurpy and difficult to follow because his top lip rode up on the swollen gums that surrounded the base of his two front teeth. The firm shiny flesh around the roots looked strained.

"I'm Rodney".

His breath offended me. Everything about him offended me. I'd signed up for this big brother thing with the hope that I'd get to bond with a kid, but all I wanted was to get away from this one.

It didn't take long to discover that Rodney was hard to be around. Always in my space. Always talking. Always touching.

If I stopped walking he'd bump into me. If I tried to talk, he'd interrupt me. If I held food, he'd reach out and grab at it.

He'd say, "Can I have a french-fry?" and I'd think, "You touched them, have them all."

My anxiety was off the charts, and I wanted to quit him. But I soldiered on because I'd already bragged that I was going to be a big brother, and the embarrassment would have been overwhelming. People wouldn't understand.

I was halfway through the summer and still going through the motions when Rodney asked for a ride home.

According to the program agreement, he was supposed to ride his bike, and I wasn't supposed to drive him anywhere, which had been a relief. But there he was, pacing, as he always did when he was stressed, asking me to put his bike in the trunk.

Saliva bubbled out with his words, hands shaking as

he spoke. "Can you? I forgot I was supposed to be home early. My mom'll be so mad. Please?"

I'd already done my two hours.

"How far do you live?"

"I don't know, not far. Come on, please."

At this point, he actually looked me in the eyes.

"Sure. Okay. I don't have to be anywhere. But only this once. I can't do it every week or anything."

He ran for the passenger door as I lifted the bike into the back. When I climbed in, I turned the air on high and rolled all the windows down. He pointed the way and we headed off to Rodney-town.

As we drove, I was feeling pretty good about myself. I was like Gandhi. Or even Jesus.

I began humming John Lennon's "Imagine".

If only there were others like me in the world. There'd be no need for greed or hunger. There'd be a brotherhood of man. Imagine all the people, living life like me. Mm-mmmm, mm-mm-mm.

About ten minutes later he pointed to a small house on the right. I pulled in, trying to aim my tires onto the concrete strips that stood for the drive. There was no grass, just dirt, and weeds long enough to scrape the underside of my car. I pulled to a stop behind an old van with duct taped plastic instead of glass in its back window.

As I put it in park, I took in the house. The front screen

door hung cockeyed from one hinge, matching the angle of everything else. The place looked as if some careless giant on a long journey had stopped to rest by sitting on the roof, causing the whole single story structure to sag to the right.

"Well there you go Rodney, home at last."

I was always tempted to call him "Rod," because he reminded me of my favorite TV show, *The Twilight Zone*, which was hosted by Rod Serling. My Rodney, however, was more like the show than the host.

I'd mentioned Mr. Serling to him once, and he said, "We don't have TV."

I figured this was because his mom didn't want the media polluting her kids' minds. But now, looking at the trash that had blown up and was trapped under the ailing bushes, pollution didn't seem like something she worried much about.

"Thanks for the ride." He took a deep breath as he swung his legs out the door. He seemed reluctant to get out of the car.

"You're welcome."

He sat there.

I said, "Okay, see you next Tuesday."

He turned back to me.

"Wanna come in and meet my mom?"

"Ah man I'd love to, but I've got a lot to do."

"But you said you didn't have nothing to do."

Busted.

"Well, yea. But I've got errands and stuff."

I could tell I'd hurt his feelings.

"Tell you what, how 'bout I come in for just a quick minute."

His oily cheeks rose into a smile and I felt better about myself.

Mother Teresa and I would have been friends if we lived closer.

"Awesome!" he said, jumping out of the car. He ran around and was waiting for me by the time I stood. He had done this with such excitement that he'd forgotten to close his door, which he noticed before I did.

"Oh, sorry." He ran back around and closed it gently, as though trying to keep our arrival a secret. I found myself doing the same.

We walked over clumps of weeds toward the house. I figured his mom was going to be pretty grateful to meet me.

When he swung the screen door, its hinge let out a complaining shriek, as if begging to be relieved of its solitary duty. The noon sunlight glinted against the white trim around the door, but because of its steep angle, failed to penetrate the rectangular hole that led into the house.

I stepped inside.

My eyes took a moment to adjust. My nose did not. The odor was so strong it had flavor.

As the gloom turned into living room, I saw piles of newspapers, magazines and boxes all around the walls. Hundreds of them, more thrown than stacked. The pale walls were bare, except for handprints, and sitting between an old couch and a ragged recliner was the only rug in the space. It was oval, and in several places the concrete floor was visible between its spiral rings.

The recliner was the type with a handle on the side. Rust held it in the reclined position, with its worn material barely clinging, hanging tattered, torn and dusty.

To my right were two open doors. The first led to a bedroom, its floor covered with piles of stained clothes and open boxes of everything from old clock radios to plastic picture frames and balls of tin foil. Rodney's mom was a hoarder. She had turned this single bedroom home into a secret vault for her worthless treasures.

The second door led to a bathroom that boasted the only color in the place. Its shower curtain held bright yellow and red cartoon birds with open wings soaring against a sky-blue background.

The far left corner of the living room revealed the edge of a kitchenette table, piled high with junk. Two metal tube chairs were visible from where I stood, each with dull stretched-plastic seats. I assumed that behind the wall was the kitchen.

Something scratched itself against the back of my mind. A question. I turned to ask, and saw Rodney pulling the screen door handle up, in order to prop its aluminum frame within the jam.

"How many brothers and sisters did you say you have?"

"Five."

He smiled, oblivious to the fact that his house was explaining more about him in that moment than a thousand conversations could have.

"Where do you all sleep?"

"We take turns on the couch." He whispered, "The recliner's the best place cause you don't have to share it, unless my mom gets sick of the baby. The rest of us sleep on the rug."

Just then his mom came from behind the kitchen wall. She had a bigheaded naked baby clinging to her hip, and a frightened toddler clutching the side of her black Led Zeppelin t-shirt with a tiny fist.

She reached back and shoved the little girl away.

She snapped, "Get off me!" as the girl stumbled back toward the corner, lip quivering.

"And stop crying, or I'll make you cry harder. You know I will."

The little girl looked down.

I attempted a polite smile as the woman looked our way.

Rodney had moved in front of me, his small shoulders tensed. Perhaps he'd been hoping for a different, less agitated version of his mom. A child can slip into the hope that maybe the few happy moments they've know will multiply, rather than disappear.

The hot air thickened around us, as if it were an omen, forecasting what lay ahead.

I didn't know what to do.

She looked at Rodney as if I was a ghost that only he could see. Her gray eyes held a hammock of darkened skin slung below. Bleached hair was tattered, reaching to her shoulders, and when she parted her lips to begin yelling at Rodney, they exposed the heredity behind her son's teeth. Hers were as big as his, but they put no limit on her ability to use profanity.

Her words were the harshest I'd ever heard.

I felt the lump in my chest first, followed by the heat and hint of tears in the corners of my eyes. I wanted to turn and run, collecting Rodney and his little sister in my arms as I did. I wanted to kick my way through the broken screen door of this broken house where this broken woman had been allowed to bring children into the world so she could break them too.

I just stood there.

The lump moved to my throat.

Her volume grew as she crossed the room toward the bedroom. She was saying something about knowing this stupid big brother thing was going to mess with her schedule and that she was even stupider than Rodney for letting him sign up.

She was difficult to follow because vulgarity bisected every sentence and my ears drummed with my own heartbeat.

Somehow timid and loud at the same time, Rodney interrupted as she took a breath between racial slurs and an expletive that began with the word "Mother."

Tragic irony.

"Mom."

"What!"

"This is my big brother Tyler." His words trailed off toward the end.

"Hi." She managed a slither of a smile, a half nod and then, "Get your lazy ass sister in the van cause I got to take you all to the damn store."

She was oblivious to the embarrassment she should have felt. She stormed into her room, mumbling something about cigarettes, and slammed the door.

I looked down at Rodney. His legs were locked, his arms stiff at his sides with fingers working over each thumb. He rocked from side to side with his head up, and his eyes looking down. Barely balancing on his bottom eyelashes were huge tears.

I could feel the heat of embarrassment coming off him. He blinked and the tears rolled through the dirt on his cheeks, leaving a trail of pink flesh. They seemed to hurry as they went, rushing for safety to the corners of his mouth. When he spoke, they were spit from his lips and scattered on the floor. It seemed there was no refuge anywhere in this dark place.

I still didn't know what to do, so I stupidly opened my mouth, "Hey Rodney, I guess I should maybe go."

He was already talking. "I'm such an idiot. I'm so stupid!"

Self-loathing is an airborne disease, and the stale atmosphere was full of it. Rodney's little sister moved and sat under a kitchen chair.

"No you're not Buddy."

He began his pacing. Two steps this way. Two that. And repeat.

His sister began a muffled cry and he seemed immune to the sound.

"No Rodney..." but he interrupted.

"No." More tears flew. "I should a known. My mom's like this a lot now and I'm such an idiot to bring you in here." He kept his voice low.

I didn't know what else to do so I bent and hugged him

so he could no longer look in my eyes. This was the first time I'd initiated physical contact since I'd reluctantly shaken his hand when we first met five weeks earlier.

My brain was constricted by my emotions. All I could think to do was to get out before I began to cry. I didn't want to cause him more embarrassment.

Still bent I patted his back and said, "It's okay Buddy, it's okay." Sometimes we repeat ourselves when we don't know what else to say. He hugged me back and began to sob, and so did his sister beneath her chair.

I could feel his mom's presence behind the bedroom door, and for fear that she'd open it and spill her anger again, I rushed the hug more than I should have.

As I stood, I glanced toward the little girl who was unsuccessfully trying to stifle her crying. She climbed out from her shelter and moved toward me with a wet face. She held her breath, reached for my leg, and clung to it with her cheek pressed against the outside of my thigh. Her little eyes looked up at mine as though she'd never seen a grown-up hug anyone before.

I patted her head. There was heat coming through her soft hair.

I needed to get out of there. I'd figure out what to do about all this later. But then was surprised by the sound of my own voice.

"Hey Rodney, what are you doing tomorrow?"

Rodney was wiping his nose on his forearm. I must have surprised him because all he could muster was, "Huh?"

I asked again and tried to smile. The lump in my throat felt malignant.

"I'm not doing anything."

As he spoke, both palms ran down his wet cheeks and directly onto his shirt to be blotted. My question had distracted him.

"How come you want to know about tomorrow?"

"Well, I was just wondering if maybe you wanted to hang out together."

"Are you kidding?" Snot ran onto his top lip. "Sure I wanna!" He tilted his head. "But wait. If I see you tomorrow, do I still get to see you next Tuesday?" He wiped at his mouth with the back of his hand.

I nodded and said, "Yea, of course."

His eyes grew large, pulling the corners of his mouth into a smile. "I can't believe I get to see you twice this week. This is awesome!"

I nodded again, afraid to speak for fear I'd lose control. I glanced at the bedroom door and could hear the muffled sounds of the complaining baby.

He grabbed my forearm with a wet hand and asked, "What do ya wanna do tomorrow?"

Deep breath. I was still stroking his little sister's hair,

her face still pressed against my leg.

"I don't know. What do you want to do?"

"You kidding? I get to pick?"

I'd always been the one to choose, to be sure we'd be done in two hours.

"Can we go to the beach? I never get to go to the beach."

"Sure, that sounds great."

I was barely hanging on.

His smile grew and was even bigger than his teeth.

"I better go ask my mom."

I nodded, "Yea, I'll wait."

I whispered a prayer as I watched him gently knock and slip inside the door. He looked like a ferret sliding into a snake hole.

When he came out he was transformed. He bounced toward me like Tigger from one of those Winnie the Pooh stories.

"She said yes! We're goin' to the beach!" He was trying not to shout.

His hands were clutching each other, as if holding onto a miracle.

"That's awesome Buddy." As I began to move to the door, the little girl grabbed my hand. She never even bothered to wipe the tears from her face.

"Oh, but Tyler..." He was hard to understand because of his excitement. "She says you have to bring me a towel.

Can you bring me one cause we don't have extras. She says you have to drive me and get me at ten and drop me at one or I can't go. So can we still do it?"

This was the first moment I felt something like love toward him.

"Sure, it all sounds great."

We were outside now, and the sunshine embarrassed me. I didn't know why.

"Is it okay if I wear my cut-offs 'cause I don't have trunks?"

"Sure. No worries. We'll have fun."

I bent into my car and hugged his little sister from my seat. She didn't want to let go until he grabbed her hand. She hugged at his wrist, her face now pressed against his forearm. She stared at me, and I couldn't read her expression.

As I backed out I looked over at them and Rodney was still talking.

"I'm going to the beach." There was a song in his voice.

He always waved goodbye in the same way. A wave, a point in my direction, a wave, then another point, and so on. This time as he pointed he bent at the waist, as if to add emphasis, "We're going to the beach! Bye Tyler. We're going to the beach!"

His little sister waved too, but just with her fingers. Open, close. Open, close. She looked from me to Rodney and then back again.

Before I was halfway down the block, the lump in my throat metastasized. They were still waving in my rearview mirror when my emotions erupted from my mouth and eyes and nose, and heaved within my chest.

I now knew why Rodney was the way he was.

I also knew something new about myself.

His mom had been a mirror, held at just the right angle to show the lumps of pride and selfishness pushing out below my well-groomed arrogance. At least she was open about her self-obsession. Mine was perhaps uglier, because I hid it under self-righteousness.

I listened to the click-click-click of my blinker at the stop sign and knew that I hadn't become a big brother in order to love a kid; I'd signed up just so I could feel like the kind of person who would be a big brother. Rodney had just been a prop, not a person. I'd been using him to make myself feel better about me.

It's possible to be involved in a great thing and miss the whole point.

As I turned left, I decided to see Rodney twice a week, and let him decide what we'd do each time. It wasn't much, but it was done with a new heart.

And with that, I began to love him. Not with the kind of love that we drag into our own gut from obligation, but with the weightless kind that has wings, and brings affection in its grasp.

I think we end up loving the ones we serve.

And Rodney loved me back with even greater abundance. It spilled from him every time he saw me and ran up to hug me, pressing his dirty cheek against the stomach of my t-shirt.

For the rest of that summer, Rodney chose the beach every week, and I got a pretty great tan.

Twice, his mom let us bring his little sister. She didn't talk much, but liked holding my hand and digging holes with me in the sand. Her name was Grace, and I hoped that one day she would be able to find some.

*   *   *

On my last night in Florida, Rodney and I were back in that same stark room where we'd first met. It was a party for all the brothers from the program. I gave him a soccer ball and a toothbrush as a goodbye present. He was excited about both, which was good because at one point he showed me how he could stick a cupcake on his teeth and hold it there with no hands. He was very proud of this.

At 8 p.m. he disappeared. When he came back, he was pacing.

"I can't believe it!" He spit the words out, his forehead

furrowed into his eyebrows.

"My mom's outside and says I have to go and I told her that the party isn't over but she says I have to go or there'll be big trouble."

I wasn't ready to say goodbye.

"I begged her but she didn't care."

His shoulders slumped and his hands began working each other.

"So I have to go now."

The lump was back.

"You still leaving tomorrow morning?"

"Yea Buddy, I fly at 6:30."

"Any way you can stay?"

"I wish there was but I've got to get to my teaching job in California. School starts the day after tomorrow. Oh man, I'm not ready to say goodbye."

"Me neither."

But then his eyes brightened. His voice was excited.

"Guess what?"

"What?"

"I wrote you a note."

"You what?"

"I wrote you a note. Wanna see it?"

"Yea, of course!"

He grabbed into his pocket and pulled out a crumpled piece of notebook paper. His toothbrush fell on the floor.

He bent, shoved it into his back pocket, flattened the note against his chest, folded it and held it out.

Every upward muscle in his face was at work.

I reached to take the note, but he wouldn't let it go.

We both stood there holding it between us.

"Want me to tell you what it says?"

"Um. Yea. Sure. Tell me."

He seemed to grow taller. I smiled, my vision getting blurry.

"It says, 'Tyler.'"

He caught himself, "No, it says, 'Dear Tyler.'"

Through the blur I could see his eyes shining.

"Then it says, 'Thank you for loving me. Rodney.'"

He let go and said, "That's all" and shrugged.

I grabbed and lifted him. His feet dangling as we hugged.

"I love you too, Buddy."

As I put him down, I heard his toothbrush hit on the floor beneath him. His foot landed on it, so he picked it up and said, "I'll use this toothbrush forever. I promise."

Then he stuck it in his mouth.

He hugged me again, and turned away. When he reached the door he stopped and waved, pointed, waved again, took the toothbrush out of his mouth, pointed it at me and yelled, "Maybe you could read your note on the plane tomorrow."

Then he was gone.

*　　　*　　　*

It's tough to stay in touch with a kid when he doesn't have a phone and moves a lot.

Nine years later I was back in Tampa to speak at a conference. They put me up in a fancy hotel, and when I asked the concierge if there was a Denny's nearby, he looked down his long nose at me and said there were a number of fine restaurants right there within the resort.

I looked back up his long nose, leaned in a bit, and spoke truth into his life.

"Sir, if you've never dipped grilled cheese into tomato soup at Denny's, you've never lived."

He waved the back of his hand toward the door and indicated that there was a Denny's just down the street next to a Motel 6.

He sniffed and said, "Those kinds of places usually go together."

I invited him to join me and he turned away with a snort, which made me smile all the way to the street. If he lived in a zoo, I think I'd just sit and watch him for hours and tap on the glass a lot knowing it would annoy him.

As I turned right along the sidewalk, someone behind

me yelled, "Tyler?"

I looked back, and about twenty yards away there were four people about to climb into a car. I didn't recognize them, so I turned and kept walking toward my soup and sandwich.

Again, "Tyler, is that you?"

I turned and still didn't recognize them.

"Tyler Durman?"

It was a tall skinny guy pointing at me. And then I saw his teeth.

"Rodney?"

He came running, dragging a girl by the hand, caveman style. He let her go and threw himself into me. Her momentum took her right past.

It was Rodney. My Rodney. And he was clean. He was in college. He was articulate. He had sideburns, and his teeth were clean.

He was holding a girl's hand! And it appeared to be voluntary.

I couldn't believe it was him.

I met his girlfriend Melissa, found out they were going out to dinner with her parents who waited back at the car. He was nervous, but wasn't pacing. He told me Grace was doing great in middle school, and we exchanged contact information and hugged goodbye like we'd done years earlier. Only this time he lifted me.

It had all happened so fast.

As they turned to walk back to the car, I overheard him say something to Melissa in a half whisper. He sort of pointed back over his shoulder toward me and after all those years said, "That's the guy I told you about."

Imagine that.

Mm-mmmm, mm-mm-mm.

Running

Nobody liked Eddie Ribaldi. He was mean and the only kid in seventh grade without friends.

What amazed me most was that no one ever made fun of his hands. While his thin frame looked normal, hanging below his elbows were immense forearms, which extended into hands that were so large they looked as if they'd been stolen from a heavy adult.

Picture Popeye without the anchor tattoos.

His hands fascinated me. I marveled whenever he picked up a pencil or turned a page and I felt the breeze. I knew it was rude, but it was hard not to stare because how often do you get to sit next to an actual flesh and blood cartoon character in class?

The skin was stretched so tight that I wondered more than once what would happen if he punctured himself. I pictured him flying backwards around the room like a balloon.

Once I stole a peace sign button from my brother and put it on the corner of my desk where I knew Eddie would grab it. I watched with great disappointment as he successfully pinned it to his t-shirt without incident.

In all these moments of fascination, I'd never once guessed that the day would come when those hands would hold the power to ruin my life.

*   *   *

It all happened in an instant. Suddenly I found myself chasing him across the blacktop toward the classroom doors, knowing that I had to catch him before he reached the building.

My future depended on it.

I was gaining on him because my legs were longer and my motivation was stronger. I needed to get back what he held in those round fingers of his.

Desperation pounded in my chest and he was just an arms length away now. I stretched for the back of his shirt, my fingertips straining, but they only grazed the smiley face logo that was staring back at me. The attempt had cost me a stride.

A few more paces and I stretched out again, but again my hand came back empty.

My breathing was louder now, and the logo looked like a goblin mocking me as it rocked from side to side. Anxiety mingled with the scent of the hot pavement below my high-tops as I leaned further forward, almost too far this time, nearly falling as Eddie darted to one side and gained some distance.

Smaller kids scattered from our path as I turned and caught up to him again. The panic moved to my throat and with each backswing of his arm, I could see that huge fist clamped tight around what he'd stolen.

I had to stop him before it was too late.

It had all began that morning, just before I got into the car for my second day of seventh grade. Though I knew I shouldn't have, I'd slipped my knife into the front pocket of my jeans as I left my room and hurried out to climb into the backseat.

"Probably won't even show anyone," I figured. It was exciting just to feel the weight of it there in my pocket.

But like Poe's Tell-Tale Heart, as the minutes past, it seemed to shout to my mom and later to my teachers that it was there, hidden in denim. It whispered privately to me with the voice of playmate and enemy. One moment thrilling, the next bringing the dread of being found out.

I knew there would be severe consequences if any teacher discovered it. I'd be suspended. Maybe even expelled. And that was nothing compared to what would happen to me when I got home.

Concealed there in my pocket, it taunted, daring me to pull it out into the light. I fumbled with it between my fingers. It was all I could think about. And then it found its opportunity during second period.

The older substitute teacher with the pleasant smile and weak demeanor took us all outside for free time on the playground.

Free time isn't always a gift when you're hiding something.

And there, near the back corner, by the fence, surrounded by my buddies, I said it.

"You guys want to see what's in my pocket?"

New volumes of blood rushed through me as I pulled the knife out and flicked it open. When the sun hit the stainless steel blade it was glorious.

Everyone wanted to hold it.

I'd never chanced such punishment. No one in my family had. My older brother and sisters had never brought a weapon to school or risked offending my parents with such blatant disregard. I was drunk with the power of it.

With two beats of my pulse, both the knife and the situation were out of my hands. We were taking turns throwing to see if we could stick it in the dirt at the edge of the blacktop.

"Let's play chicken." The words were out of my mouth before I knew they were mine. We started aiming near one another's feet, each trying to avoid the urge to flinch. The blade slid in and out of earth as more boys were drawn to the action. It was a feeding frenzy and I was at the center.

I was the ringleader. An outlaw. Invincible.

Wrong.

My twelve-year-old world hit the fan as Edward Chubby Hands ran up, grabbed my knife and ran away with it.

"Tyler's got a knife, Tyler's got a knife!"

My jaw dropped and my cockiness fell hard to the punctured dirt. It split into shards of panic as I realized that he held more than my knife in those fingers of his.

I took off after him and it was then, as I began the chase, that clarity forced her way into my little brain. "Hey Stupid! A knife is a dangerous thing when you throw it around a playground. Kids can get hurt."

I knew these things, but I just hadn't thought it would come to this.

No fool ever does.

Everything became visceral, as primal instinct took over. I was getting closer. Just a few more strides. Must get him before he gets inside.

Now!

I threw myself at the back of his heels just as he crossed the painted home plate of the kickball field. As we fell, both my jeans and the skin on my knees tore as they met blacktop. Gravel ground into flesh.

I didn't notice the pain till later because I was focused on my knife as it fell at the feet of Miss Castillo, the sour-faced, nature-loving art teacher. We called her, "Miss Hug-A-Tree-O", and the sight of her jump-started my mind.

Oh God please, anyone but her! Everyone knew she was weird and mean. She'd never even been married, even though she was totally old. She was like twenty-eight or something. She liked trees and clouds and stuff. Every day she wore a huge peace sign slung around her neck, swinging against tie-dye. She hated war and violence, which is why I suspected I wouldn't be getting extra-credit in art class for tackling the school outcast, on pavement, as he was running for his life with my open knife in his hand.

The expression on her face verified my suspicion.

She snatched up the knife and caught my arm. I knew where she was dragging me, but the Principal's Office scared me less than knowing that soon I'd have to walk into the kitchen of my own home.

In that moment I knew that my life had come to irreparable ruin. All safety was gone, and I was convinced that the ones I loved and needed the most were about to reject me – forever.

These are always the first lies of failure.

I found myself walking toward my house at 10:45 in the morning, after being suspended from seventh grade. I'd been kicked out. Banished. Deemed unfit to be in the presence of other kids.

I cried the whole way, both from guilt for the immediate past, and fear for the immediate future.

Because Dawn, the cute girl at school, had seen me crying in the office, I knew that by now my weakness would be the talk of the cafeteria. I also knew that in the house up ahead, I was about to face parents who'd regret I shared their last name.

Both my rock and my hard place had a street address.

My mom was on the phone with the Principal when I walked through the kitchen door. The timing sucked. She had no space to reflect. Her youngest had brought a weapon to school, was standing in front of her, she'd just found out, and it wasn't even eleven in the morning yet. Her particular shade of red warned me that what was coming wouldn't involve milk and cookies.

Her lecture ended with, "Go to your room and wait till your father gets home." My fear started throbbing. The worst was yet to come.

6 p.m. crept up to the house like a dark shadow, full of

menace. I heard it arrive with the opening of the garage door. He was home. His hands were powerful, and they were coming for me. I began to sweat as I heard him ascend the stairs from the basement, and it was then that I lost touch with reality.

Though my father had never lost control or raised his hand to me in anger, imaginings, like the ones that gripped me after a nightmare, started to compound my fear.

I listened at my door. Was that a chain he was dragging? I heard the muffled sounds of his conspiratorial conversation with my mom. He walked up and waited on the other side of the final barrier between us, and I shrank back because I could hear him breathing the septic air of crude anger.

I pictured him standing there with a machete.

Here it was. An eye for an eye and a blade for a blade.

The pocket door slid open slowly and my lungs lost their ability to exhale. I didn't move and for a moment couldn't look. He stood there staring at me until I did. Without speaking, he unfurled one of his muscular python-like fingers and motioned me to follow.

As he turned I noticed that he had no chain, no machete, only car keys. That's when I figured he was taking me to one of those "camps" for troubled kids who are no longer allowed to live at home.

Rejection and abandonment are any child's greatest fear, and I knew I had brought them both on myself.

Everything kicked into slow motion, and the walk down to the garage seemed to take hours. I was numb. All hope was gone.

Dead boy walking.

This was it. I said a silent goodbye to everything we went past, knowing I'd never see it again. I'd rather have faced the Principal another time, or even a whole cafeteria of snickering kids, than the silence of this looming hulk that was Father. He was walking in front of me with his head tilted to one side like Quasimodo.

The windows beckoned, whispering, "Pssst, use us. Leap from our sill. Run! It's your only hope." But I was too terrified to make a break.

When we got to the garage he made me get in the driver's side. He had the keys and went around and opened the passenger door and leaned in. It was then that I noticed he hadn't opened the garage door, and the dreadful thought exploded in my brain.

Death by asphyxiation!

He bent his huge frame into the car and sat beside me. After closing his door, he stared at the garage wall in front of us and said nothing. You could have heard a drop of sweat hit the fake leather upholstery. When he turned to face me, I sort of flinched.

Here it comes. I was about to be banished, sent away, given proof that I'd out pushed every boundary of his patience.

I had lost my home.

My short and shallow breathing ceased as I pressed my lips together.

It's been forty years since that moment, and I can still remember the pacing of each word.

"Before you tell me what happened today, I want you to know that I love you no matter what you do. Nothing you've ever done, or will ever do, could change how much I love you."

Huh? Wow! What just happened?

Brain bewildered.

Breathing again.

He's not going to kill, dismember or discard me? I'm not going to have to do everyone's chores?

A brief pause. I looked at the wall.

I looked back at him. He was still looking at me.

He smiled.

I smiled, sort of.

I looked at the wall again and tried to think.

As I remember that moment now, I'm struck by something significant. Though I didn't know it at the time, his words had formed the two most profound sentences I would ever hear. They were teaching me that

I was safe, in spite of being flawed. That I had somewhere to run.

I suppose we're all going to run someplace when we fail.

"So you're not mad?"

"No, I'm pretty mad."

"So how come you're not yelling?"

"Do I ever yell?"

"Just that time Barry said, 'I'm not doing it, that's Mom's job."

He smiled, "I forgot about that."

"That was cool! I liked it when you yelled at him."

"I'm sure you did, but I brought you out here because I want tell you a story that might help you understand why I'm not yelling now."

"Is it about when you were a kid?"

"Yup."

"Did you have to walk to school in the snow?"

He laughed, "There's no snow in this story."

"Okay then."

"I know you didn't spend a lot of time with your grandma, because she lived in England, but she could be pretty negative."

"I remember when she visited and yelled at Daryl and me because we were giggling at the table and couldn't stop. She got so mad she sent us to bed without eating, but then mom got home and they had this big fight about it."

"Mom was sticking up for you."

"Yeah, that was cool too!"

"Well here's the story. When I was about ten, two of my friends invited me to go to the municipal baths after school."

"That's creepy!"

"What?"

"They wanted to take a bath with you!"

"No, that's just what they call indoor community pools in England."

"That's weird."

"No, England just has a different culture."

"Still, they should know what a bath is."

"The point is I'd never been in a pool before."

"How come? Did you live in the ghetto or something?"

"No. Just let me tell the story, okay?"

"Okay."

"So there were two pools, and one was for kids. I remember being amazed at the smell of the air and the water. It was a whole new world to me. The windows were all fogged up."

"Can I ask a question?"

Exhale. "Sure."

"Does this have to do with me getting suspended?"

"Yes."

"Can I have my knife back?"

He sighed. "Please just let me tell this story."

"Okay."

"So my friends jumped into the shallow end of the pool, which it turns out was only about two-and-a-half feet deep. I didn't know it was that shallow because they tucked up their legs to make splashes."

"Cannonballs."

"Yup. So when I jumped in, because I didn't know what I was doing, I landed with my legs strait and my knees locked. When I hit the bottom I heard this popping sound, and pain exploded in my back. It ran down both legs and I couldn't breathe. Years later a doctor said that one of my vertebrae had been pushed out of place, and I'd ruptured two discs."

"What's a vertebrae again?"

"Do you listen in school?"

"Sometimes. But sometimes I just stare at Dawn."

"Who?"

"Dawn. She's really great looking! She has brown hair and..."

He held up his hand and took a deep breath. "Vertebrae are those bones that go down your back, and your spinal cord runs through them. It's where most of your nerves are. Anyway, you know how my back hurts all the time?"

"Yeah."

"Well the doctors say that when I landed in the pool, my spinal cord was bent and got squeezed in two places."

"You shouldn't have jumped in the shallow end like that."

"Thank you, I know that now."

"So what happened?"

"I just sort of rolled out of the water and lay there on my side for a while. It took time before I could breathe, and eventually the pain settled down enough so I could walk home. The whole time I was afraid because I knew my mom was going to yell at me."

"Weren't you supposed to be at the pool?"

"No, she knew I was going, but she criticized me anytime I did something she thought was dumb."

"But I don't get it. Why couldn't the doctor fix your back?"

"Well, that's why I'm telling you this story. I never went to the doctor back then because I never told my mom what happened. I couldn't face her because I knew she'd be angry and say I was careless or should be more observant or something."

"So is that why we don't have a pool?"

"No, that's because pools are expensive."

"Do you think we could afford one of those above the ground pools?"

He shook his head and closed his eyes for a second.

"Anyway, I told you this story because when your mom and I started having kids, I decided I never wanted any of you to feel the way I did that day."

"Yeah, we have good backs."

"I'm not talking about your backs. I just want you to feel like you can come home and be honest, even when you make a mistake."

"So you're saying that since grandma was mean to you, I'm not in trouble for getting suspended, right?"

"No, you're in a lot of trouble, but we'll talk about that tomorrow. I just want you to know that even though you did this thing today, I still love you and you can always come to me no matter what. Okay?"

"Okay."

"So you understand?"

"I think so."

"Good."

We both turned and looked at the wall. When I looked back at him he was smiling and I watched him for a moment.

"Thanks for not yelling at me."

He seemed to be focused on something far away, and I thought he hadn't heard. But then, still smiling and without turning his head, he said, "You're welcome."

It seems to me now that redemption has a way of

folding itself back over time, so that while I was receiving grace in that car, the child that my dad had been, was accepting it somewhere in the past.

We sat together in silence for a little while and it felt comfortable.

Then I said, "So I still have a question."

"What's that?"

"Does this mean I get my knife back?"

"Don't push it Son."

"Okay. But Mom says I have to say I'm sorry to Eddie. Do I?"

"What do you think?"

"Yeah, I know."

Another pause.

"You should see his hands Dad. They're bigger than yours! Sometimes I just stare!"

He sighed again. I figured it was because his back was hurting.

Another moment and then, "Dad?"

"Yeah?"

"If you love me so much, how come I don't get my knife back?"

He just got out of the car and went inside, shaking his head the whole way.

On Slanted Hill

The ground was angled and dusty. As I walked with him down the path I smiled because this wasn't what I'd expected. No palms. No springs. I'd been fooled by the name.

"We'd love you to come and tell some of your stories at our school this August."

He wasn't what I'd expected either. When he called, his raspy voice had brought to mind the image of a young Clint Eastwood from one of those old cowboy movies.

"Our students need to learn how to treat each other." His words squeezed past dry vocal cords. "I'm trying to teach them to look past their differences and take care of each other."

Clint Eastwood with a compassionate heart. I liked him for that, so I told him I'd come.

Now, as I followed his round little body to the football

stadium, I could see that the only thing he had in common with a cowboy was his need for a hat. The sun had reached through his thinning hair to do its damaging work.

"It's a bit hot, but us desert folk are used to it."

A bit hot? It was 106 degrees. Even Satan wouldn't come near this place in August. My shirt had already soaked its way into my back. Skin and cotton bewildered as the boundary between them blurred.

He had scheduled the program to be outside because it was the only place he could fit all his students at once. There was no shade, and no breeze, so I smiled politely and watched 1,700 high school students sizzle their way onto the cement seats.

He took the microphone and introduced me, and I realized that while I'd been wrong about his appearance, I'd been right about his heart. You could feel his love for these teenagers in the way he spoke to them. His rounded shoulders seemed to reach downward in an attempt to surround a chest that would otherwise burst with kindness. These were tough kids, many of them gang members, and yet the sincerity of his voice quieted them.

Or maybe it was the heat.

When I stood to speak, 3,400 eyes begged, "Mister, please don't take the whole hour. It's already been three whole minutes. I'm done on this side, flip me over."

I couldn't blame them; I didn't want to be there either.

I just wanted to get this one behind me and get to my car. I looked over at their principal and he smiled, giving me a giddy thumbs up with his shoulders all pulled up to his ears. Couldn't he smell the burning flesh? Had he never heard the word melanoma? But he still had my check growing damp in one of his pockets, so I smiled back, pretending to be excited at the opportunity to change lives with my words.

The sixty minutes trickled past like taffy dripping down a hot road. When the final applause came it seemed sincere, though it was probably because I'd finally shut up.

And I was done.

Ah!

After a wet hug from my non-cowboy, his eyes moist with gratitude, I headed up the hill for the air-conditioned cockpit of my rental car, my soggy check slipped into my soaked shirt pocket. Cooler places were calling so I walked with keys in hand and eyes to the ground so no one would slow my escape.

I was halfway up the hill when I heard her voice. She said seven words that I hoped were meant for someone else, but when I glanced back she was following me, and she was alone.

"There's something I need to tell you."

I squeezed out a smile and invited her to join me in the shade of a nearby tree where the temperature was only ninety-nine.

That's when I noticed her eyes. I'd missed what was in them at first. They were a deep well of dark and old sorrow. The kind that's only fit for someone who's been alive much longer than she had, and been worn down by the weight of long and permanent heartache. I found myself teetering there, on the edge of her sadness, trying not to fall in.

Just then, my new friend with the rounded shoulders walked past and in the slow motion of that moment, caught my eye and smiled as though he'd previously sensed her pain and was grateful she'd chosen to talk to me.

She said it again. This time with a smaller voice and a hint of tears, "There's something I need to tell you."

Her eyes were down and she rocked just slightly. I could tell she wasn't used to letting anyone see her feelings.

"What's your name?"

"Moema." Her voice was quiet, as if apologizing.

"That's pretty. I've never heard that name before."

She looked up. "It's Native American."

"Do you know what it means?" I asked.

"It means Sweet One."

And she was.

She asked if she could tell me something she'd never

told anyone before. A secret she'd kept since she was six. Over half her life.

I slipped my keys into a pocket as she began to turn hers in the door to her past. I could see that she was fumbling with the lock.

Why she chose that day to reveal the thing, I can't tell. Why she'd chosen me to watch as she dragged the secret into the sunlight, I'm not sure. But as she began to speak, for the first time that day I was glad I had come.

She started by saying that she hadn't been able to tell anyone because she was afraid. "I've tried to tell my mom a thousand times."

With this, her tears turned to sobs and she collapsed forward, falling into me, her legs too weak to carry the weight of all those moments come together in this one.

I caught her and her next words were moaned against my chest, "I'm so scared."

She shook.

Terrified of rejection, her sixteen years had not yet taught her that real safety is only possible when we come out of hiding.

Though she couldn't have known it, I had been moaning against this same truth my whole life.

I stood her up, smiled and said, "It's okay Moema, keep going."

She nodded, took a deep wet breath, and went on.

Her secret had first found life on the angled ground of another hill, not far from where we stood. It had been a Saturday, following a rare and long rain. The skies had drained themselves with such passion that the streams had become rivers and the aqueducts, torrents. The sun had pushed back the clouds at last, so their babysitter took Moema and her little brother outside for some fun.

Their play led the four- and six-year-old along the side of an aqueduct that was screaming its course nearby. There on the slope, enveloped in childhood ignorance and the sound of the hostile water, Moema and her little brother began throwing rocks and sticks into the water. They were delighted with their new plaything, unaware that it was waiting to devour any prey it could touch.

The hungry liquid had cast some bait within reach. Both kids saw it. It was a stick. Just a stick. But in the eyes of the children, it was perfect. The kind of stick aqueduct throwers dream of.

As they ran for it, the sound of the torrent drowned out their giggles – and the screams of their sitter. At precisely the same moment they lunged, grasped, and fell. Moema onto the ground, her little brother into the water, where he was inundated and vanished. She screamed, stood, turned. The blur of the sitter's dive caught the corner of her eye. And then she was alone.

She would never see either of them again.

And that was it. Her secret was born at the death of her brother. She believed that she was the killer, not the water; that she was the murderer, not the mistake.

She didn't know what to do. Jump in? Scream? Run? She was only six. Only 6. And so she screamed. No one came and she was still alone. Eventually the little dazed girl stumbled back to the street, led by the sound of her own anguish.

Her eyes were wild with fear when a car stopped. There was a nice man. A police siren. An ambulance. Faces. Questions. More faces. More questions. But none were the face of her little brother. When would he come home? He won't? Never?

Never.

After the faces disappeared, her own questions continued and became the quiet refrain that welcomed her to each emptier day.

"I was so scared, Tyler." Her voice desperate now, "I didn't want my mom to hate me. I didn't want to go to jail, so I lied and said he'd fallen in by himself!" She rocked her head back and wailed, falling into me again, her body one big tremble.

I stood there with her weight and shudders pressing into me, searching for something to say. Nothing came. All I knew was that no one's shoulders could be strong enough to carry such a weight.

I can't say how long it was before she stepped back and stood on her own, but when she did her eyes were vacant. She looked like a hollow replica of Moema. The only evidence she was still inside were her tears, which fell now without sound.

Her life had been dominated by lies: Her mother's weeping, her fault. Her parents divorce, her fault. Her dad's alcoholism, her fault.

Like some dying flower she had closed in on herself, choosing solitary confinement as her own punishment. Self-loathing and guilt had led to depression and continual thoughts of suicide. She stayed alive, she said, to save her mom from more pain.

And so, as one month dripped into the next, she lost her youth. No sleepovers, no friends, no dates. Just hollow weeks spent alone in her room. Her iPod her armor. Her black clothes her mourning.

Like every other little girl who ever became a teenager, all she really wanted was to be loved. But you can't feel loved if you don't feel known, and her pretending had made intimacy impossible.

That is until this day, while standing on a new hill, the lonely six-year-old reached out her teenage hand and dragged her secret out into the open. There on the dusty angled ground, it finally met its match. I watched it squirm. Witnessed its last twitch. Saw it die. And its death was marvelous.

Her hiding was over.

I think she expected me to echo the contempt she'd poured on herself for so long, but instead I told her the truth, and for the first time, at sixteen, Moema learned that she was not to blame. The sitter had made the tragic mistake. Gravity and inertia had taken her brother, and it wasn't her fault. She'd only been six. A little first-grader. She was innocent then, and she was innocent now.

Innocent?

Innocent.

What a beautiful word.

Moema. Sweet one. Set free.

The tears she cried now were different. They were liquid relief. The beginning of self-forgiveness.

We walked and talked, and then I encouraged her to call home, and she did. Her mom came to the school right away and we all sat together in the principal's office. She was shaking when she re-told her story, and instead of being hated, she was hugged. More tears flowed and her mom said some words of her own, "Sweetheart, it wasn't your fault. I promise!"

That moment was like watching her being born all over again. Only this time, instead of a doctor, Clint's twin was there to help the birth along. His eyes were wet again, and he poured love on that little family as though it was his last act before entering the O.K. Corral.

As he walked me out he said, "That Moema's a courageous little girl."

I nodded, "Yes she is."

We thanked each other for the day, and he put his hand on my arm and said, "It's humbling to think that you never know who's hurting, even when they're standing right in front of you."

And something in his expression told me that he was talking about me. I don't know how, but he could somehow see that I was carrying secrets of my own, and my chest swelled at the thought.

He smiled, patted my shoulder and said, "When you're ready." And I didn't know if he meant, "When I was ready to talk, someone would listen" or "When I was ready to leave, I could get into the car." So I just sort of stood there feeling dumb.

He smiled again and hugged me, so I opened my driver's door, and as I bent into the seat asked, "Would you do me a favor?"

He nodded, "Sure! Anything."

I closed the door, rolled down the window and said, "Would you mind saying, 'Do you feel lucky? Well, do ya, punk?'"

We both laughed and I drove away.

As I did, I couldn't shake his words or the thought of Moema's courage, and I knew it was time to keep the promise I'd made to myself months earlier in my outdoor shower.

My hand smelled like Purell and I took a deep breath as I reached for my phone. When my best friend answered I said, "There's something I need to tell you."

The Hero and the Target

Carlo smiled as he watched his son on the trail ahead of him, the cool October sunshine lighting the slight puffs of dust stirred by Jake's feet. The seven-year-old ambled more than walked, stopping often to pick up this stick or to throw that rock. The dawdling was okay with Carlo because the slower the day went, the better.

Since the loss of his wife, this sneaker-wearing bundle of activity walking in front of him had come to synthesize all that mattered in his new, quieter world.

Today was to be treasured. They had a backpack stuffed with drinks, the branches they'd picked up to use as walking sticks, and nothing but time to be together on their favorite hike. The giant eucalyptus trees were whispering fragrant promises of the father-son memories the day would bring.

It had only been about an hour, but the crisp air had

already been full of laughter and boy-talk about big spiders, giant snakes, and the huge mountains they'd climb together one day.

As was the tradition at this point in their hike, Jake ran ahead and disappeared around a curve where the trail carved itself into the side of a hill, becoming more ravine than pathway. Knowing why Jake had run, Carlo snuck in after him and crouched against the rock face just this side of the first curve. Flanked there by two fifteen-foot cliffs, he pictured his son doing the same around the other side of the bend.

They'd played this game before.

Smiling to himself, he waited a bit longer than usual, knowing that when he did burst around the corner, the startle would go deeper, and so would the laughter. The boy would become animated bliss. Ointment for a dad's heart.

Holding his breath, Carlo crept closer and then exploded around the curve, hands in front of hips, ready to catch as Jake fell giggling against his body. But he found nothing except dry ground.

Suspecting that Jake was hiding around the next bend, he snuck up again, waited and then jumped. But again, there were no belly laughs to greet him. The only movement was a listless dust devil doing its best to dance on a pile of small rocks.

He felt concern strum across the strings in his gut. The vibrations sending him quickly to the next bend. But again, no Jake.

They had an understanding. When they were on this trail, they were to stay near each other. Jake had never once strayed from this. Something must have happened.

The thought caused his feet and heart to move faster. He rounded the next bend, rock walls looming, and still no Jake. He called, paused, listened, but there was no answer.

He'd lost his wife and he wasn't going to lose his son. He was barely holding on as it was, and knew that more loss would crush him. Worst-case scenarios began playing in his mind. He stood there, not knowing which way to go. He shouted for Jake again.

Nothing.

He looked forward and then back, the trail in each direction bending out of sight. Remembering that it was wisest not to go too far from where he'd last seen Jake, he decided to go back to where they'd been separated. He took a step in that direction and then froze.

It was Jake's voice, and it was coming from above.

"Dad!"

Hope filled him.

Carlo's eyes darted up and what he saw splintered his short-lived relief. Jake was in mid-air, having just jumped from about eleven feet up, with a huge smile on his face.

Adrenaline flooded his muscles as he stepped forward just in time for the catch. They both crumpled to the ground, with Jake laughing and Carlo on his knees, clutching his boy to his chest.

Relief was back, but confusion and anger were crowding in. He put his hands on Jake's shoulders and moved him to arm's length.

"What were you thinking? What if I didn't catch you?"

Jake smiled, "I knew you'd catch me. You're my Dad."

*   *   *

Wow! Beautiful. When Carlo told me this story it stirred some primitive longing inside me. What an amazing thing for a son to say to his dad.

Carlo said it had been healing for him. That those words, and the simplicity of his little boy's trust, were like a flower growing in the rubble of his fallen dreams. Proof that hope was reasonable. Evidence of the beautiful gardens to come.

And he was right.

When he ended his story there was a profound silence between us. Then I said that perhaps the story also highlighted that maybe Jake wasn't the sharpest kid on the planet, given the fact that he'd jumped from eleven feet up and all.

Carlo smiled.

"Not your fault if the boy's a bit dumb," I said.

He punched me in the shoulder.

We both laughed, and as I rubbed my muscle I thought of my own sons, and how grateful I was that we're so close. But then something else struck me. Wait a minute! How come I didn't have any great father-son stories of my own? It had been six and eight years since I'd spent my three minutes contributing to the creation of each of their lives, and neither of them had given me a single story as cool as Carlo's.

I was taken aback. I'm arguably the coolest dad on the planet, they literally wouldn't exist without me, and they had given me nothing! The little takers.

Something had to be done!

I determined to put the pressure on until I got my story. I'd insist that they stand and address me as "Captain, my Captain" whenever their friends were over. And yes, I'd make them wear t-shirts to school every day with a big picture of my face on the front and the words, "My Dad, My Hero!" That'd teach them.

I was going to get my story even if I had to throw them off a cliff myself to make it possible.

And then one evening, a couple of weeks later, it

happened all by itself.

The three of us were in a Motel 6 together, just within view of Seattle's skyline, and safe beyond nightfall's fingers that were tapping at our windowpane. Yup. A Motel 6. It's cheap, but I deserve the best.

We'd been laughing and wrestling like the WWF wanna-bees that we are, and had fallen sweaty and exhausted onto the two beds that flanked the room. After a few minutes, six-year-old Paul and I moved to the carpet and sat facing each other. We were trying to shoot our bouncy ball into the empty ice bucket, which we took turns holding. He was Michael Jordan. I was Larry Bird.

Spencer, who was apparently still in the mood to be a big-time-body-slamin'-wrestler, crept in silence onto the surface of the dresser to my back. Then, still climbing with stealth, moved up onto the top of the TV, which sat about three feet behind and above my head.

He stood to his full height, picturing the chanting crowd coming to its feet as they watched him climb onto the edge of the ring. The TV beneath him was the top rope, and his jump was to be the crushing blow that would send the crowd into a frenzy as they began chanting his name.

He jumped as high as he could, with a trajectory that would bring him down directly onto my head. As he did, in mid-air, he let out a primal scream.

"Aaarrrggg!"

My startled heart leapt. I spun, and with cat-like-martial-arts-reflexes, grabbed him as he came down on top of me. And in that shard of time, just as I saw him there falling toward me, I thought to myself, "YES! The story can be mine!"

I was thrilled, and so with all the drama and feigned exasperation I could muster, I put him down in front of me, and moved him back to arm's length. With distress in my voice I asked, "Spence, what if I didn't catch you?"

He paused, he thought. I waited, I prayed.

He answered.

"Yeah, I guess that was kind-a stupid, huh?"

Chew'n and Spit'n

I love the smell of fresh sawdust and the satisfaction of hammering a nail, but I'd never make it in the world of construction. I just don't have the skills. I admire anyone who does because I think it would be pretty cool to be able to create something tangible you can drive by years later and say, "I built that."

I think it would impress the ladies.

As a speaker and writer, all I get to say about a place is, "I said words there." Not quite as manly. Even six-year-old girls say words. So do feeble old ladies and some pretty birds.

My friend Keith is so cool that he said, "Honey, I'm going to build us our dream house" and she responded, "Sounds great Babe!"

How cool is that? I can't even get a woman to call me Babe.

Because Keith has been one of my best friends for years, I spent many Saturdays at his property trying to help. I think he likes having me there because I make him laugh and always bring refreshing beverages and a bag of beef jerky.

I believe that the world would be a much happier place if we all brought snack foods wherever we go. About to get mugged on the subway? Pull out a Twinkie for the guy and I'd bet my last popsicle that he'll hug you and move on. Get pulled over by a cop who says, "Can I see your license and registration?" Just say, "Nope, but I do have a tasty cupcake I'd like to offer you."

The other day a guy in traffic told me to go and do something to myself that's physically impossible. I just smiled and waved but wished I had a warm cookie to toss him. I think shared snacks are the answer to all human friction.

I should hold public office.

So anyway, one Saturday Keith says, "Hey Tyler, you know how to tie steel?"

And I say, "Sure, what do you think, I never tied steel before? Jeeez!"

So he says, "What's tying steel?"

And I say, "Haven't got a clue."

So he says, "Yea I thought so. Come on, I'll teach you."

So I learned how to tie heavy wire around steel rods

called "rebar." They weigh a lot and are about as thick as your thumb. The reason you do this is so the rods stay together when you pour concrete in the holes for the foundation.

I felt manly.

Because Keith is one of my smartest friends it surprised me that he trusted me with the foundation of his house. It was an important job, so I worked hard and felt tough wearing my work gloves and chew'n my jerky.

When no one was looking I pretended it was chewing tobacco so I could do macho things like spit and talk to myself with a big chunk of it in my cheek.

Every once in a while Keith would stop by to inspect my work, and it seemed I was doing well. This made me happy. I felt useful.

As the day chewed its way through the hours, I kept quiet about the fact that tying steel must use muscles typing doesn't, and that my hands had begun to ache a lot with each twist and cut. But a guy can't complain about pain on a construction site without feeling like a sissy. So I just kept working.

When the trucks came and the concrete was poured, lots of the steel I'd tied toward the end of the day, fell apart.

I stood there feeling stupid as I watched Keith redo my work, while the truly manly guys who came with the trucks had to wait. This cost Keith time, which on a job site is expensive. I felt helpless and tried to stay out of the way. I could feel my ego shrinking, like other parts of me do when I swim in a cold lake.

Far worse than my hurt pride was the fact that I knew finances were tight for my friends, and this was costing them lots of money they didn't have.

Sometimes even when my motives are pure, I end up hurting the people I love.

I had to leave before Keith and the trucks were done, so I crept to my white-collar car and slid down the road, trying to be as invisible as I could.

I left some jerky on his toolbox as a first attempt at saying sorry, and left my leather gloves on the ground so he'd know he wouldn't have to ask me to stay away from the work site in the future.

It was a long week and I had a pit in my stomach. We called each other a couple of times, but our schedules never matched. Time moves slowly when you're afraid you've done damage to a friendship.

I wanted to tell him how sorry I was in person, and knew where I'd be able to find him. So the next Saturday I slunk up to the property. He was swinging one of his thick arms and banging nails into heavy lumber. His back was to me when I walked up so I just stood there feeling dumb.

When the banging stopped, I said hi. My voice sounded like a girl.

He turned, smiled, and grabbed my gloves that were tucked in the back of his tool belt, and tossed them to me. He'd been hoping I'd come.

Ah, sweet forgiveness.

I tossed him some jerky and we both set to work banging nails. We even laughed about it all later. I told him he should have known that I was just a sissy writer who isn't manly enough to be trusted with tying steel. And he said his family would have to move in with me for a while till he could afford to put on the roof, since my girly hands had made that impossible at the present time.

I think that friendship can be even more beautiful than a dream house. Even one with ceiling fans and those pretty dangly lights over the kitchen island.

Keith made me promise that I'd always tell him when something hurt, and not wait until things started falling apart before I let him in on it. Then he mumbled something about how important this was in all relationships, but I couldn't understand him on account of all the jerky in his cheek.

So I spit once into the dirt as my way of saying that I thought he was very wise.

Frogs

"Hope is the thing with feathers, that perches in the soul,
And sings the tune without the words, and never stops at all."
Emily Dickinson

Spring had reached the cul-de-sac before I had, her lazy breath moving through leaves and over fresh-cut grass.

I was putting my car in park when his blond hair caught my eye. It bounced in the sun as he burst from the front door and leapt down the two steps from the landing. Startled birds scattered as he hit the lawn at a full sprint.

Seeing his smile come at me signaled my stomach to switch to butterfly mode. Wings all fluttering inside. I pushed the door and rushed to step out as he rounded the back of the car and jumped into my arms, almost knocking me back into my seat.

My seven-year-old son, his chest against mine, there's nothing better. It'd been three weeks since my last visit, but now my heart was full again. Smelling Paul's hair and absorbing his energy made the heaviness of missing him disappear. For five years I'd been making this long journey as often as I could.

As his feet dangled in mid-air I squeezed and kissed and did all kinds of other things that little boys pretend to hate. In the midst of his giggles he was trying to talk.

"Dad. Dad! Stop! Guess what? Dad! Stop!"

Before I could give him the chance to talk, the other half of my heart came through the front door, all smiles and waves.

"Spence!" I shouted, as I started toward him, throwing Paul over my shoulder, his legs kicking. Spencer was nine, and seeing him there caused the butterflies to kick it up a notch.

This is where I belonged.

"Dad!" Paul said, his head halfway down my back. "I'm trying to show you something!"

As I set him down I noticed he was holding each hand as though cradling something fragile. Just then Laurie came through the front door. She smiled and said, "He's been pretty excited for you to get here."

She's their mom, my friend, and a beautiful person. We were divorced when our boys were small, before I was bright enough to recognize how lucky I was. She's since remarried, and along with her husband, is proof that even ashes can become seeds for beauty. Our relationship is close and deep.

As I walked toward the house, Paul bounced along beside me, talking faster than two teenage girls after a school dance.

"Dad! I caught two little green tree frogs yesterday and kept them alive so you could see them and set them free with me before they die and you can hold one but not my favorite one and you have to be careful not to squish it so do you wanna see them now Dad, do you, do you want to?"

As the frog wrangler and I stepped up onto the landing, I said hi to Laurie while I hugged Spencer. So good to have him in my arms. All the while, I was trying to show Paul how excited I was about his web-footed friends. As a former seven-year-old boy, I was aware that this was a pretty big deal.

My own dad was great in moments like this; always listening, always interested. Whether it was a frog, a soccer game, a driving test, or even the time I got beat up in the bathroom at school by the big kid named John right after I made a joke about how his name fit well into the ambiance of that particular room. John was apparently a tad sensitive about his name. And, as I found out a few months later in that same bathroom, so was his big brother Richard.

But I digress.

Paul reached out and carefully handed me my frog. Then, with his chest puffed out, showed me his favorite one. It was bright green, smaller than his pinky nail, and half the size of my frog. I could see why he loved it.

He looked up and said, "Wanna go set them free now?" I nodded, and as I stepped off the landing, turned to ask Spencer if he wanted to join us in this important conservationist endeavor.

As the words were leaving my mouth, something terrible happened. I knew this because of the anguish in Paul's scream.

"NOOOOOO!!!!!!!!"

I froze; my left foot still on the landing, my right down on the first step. Tears already streamed from Paul's eyes.

"What happened?" The words flew out of my mouth with some dead butterflies. I looked at Laurie for some hint, but she was busy asking the same question.

His little body convulsed as he tried to talk.

"You" – sob – "killed" – sob – "my" – sob – "frog!" – sob.

"No I didn't. Look Buddy, it's still here in my hand."

"Not that one!" Big breath. More tears. He pointed at my right foot.

"You stepped on mine!"

As all our eyes turned toward that foot, I whispered, "Oh God, please don't let this be!" But my prayer had come too late. I slowly lifted my foot, and there it was. Irrefutable evidence.

Frog carcass. Squished love. Round wet circle of green death.

We all looked at Paul who was still staring at his little broken friend. His face was tortured as he looked up at me and screamed it again.

"You – killed – my – frog!"

I reached for him but he turned and ran into the house, crying all the way up the stairs toward his room.

An awkward silence flowed onto the landing. We all looked at each other and then back at the wet spot. I couldn't believe it.

This moment was supposed to be happy. A sweet reunion. The thing that had kept me going for the last three weeks. I'd been there for less than one minute, and I'd already crushed my little boy's frog.

What are the odds?

The precision of the leap. The timing of the step.

That frog had to launch itself from his hand at a precise nanosecond and trajectory in order to make it possible for the little thing to land squarely in the shadow of my right foot just as I stepped off the landing.

It was impossible, but there it was, all stuck to the step.

I knew it was just a frog, but these rare times with my boys were so important to me, and Paul's words had crashed into my gut with the force of a judge's gavel.

Guilty as charged. And there was nothing I could do to fix it.

Sometimes I wish I was Jesus.

I handed Paul's other frog to Spencer.

"Take care of this for me."

He smiled, then chuckled, "You killed his frog."

"I know I did."

I looked at Laurie, motioned toward the door, and she said, "Go ahead."

As I ran up the stairs I heard Spencer's voice behind me. "Hey Dad, do you want me to kill this one too?"

Brother.

When I reached the top of the stairs, I heard Paul crying in his room, but when I looked in I couldn't see him. There was his dresser, his nightstand, his small desk, and then I heard that he'd taken refuge in the 10-inch space beneath his bed. His sadness was unrelenting as it echoed in the hollows of the box spring.

It hit me that this was the first time something he loved had died. It also struck me that there are millions of children his age experiencing true tragedy, and real loss. But pain is relative, and I knew that I needed to be careful not to diminish the validity of what he was feeling. It was real to him, so it needed to be real to me.

When I bent to look at him, I saw that he was facing

the other way, with knees drawn up. I went around to the other side, and got down on my hands and knees. As I did, he turned his back.

"Go away!"

Ouch!

I paused.

I didn't know what to do.

I'm aware that sometimes, "Go away" means, "Do you love me enough to persevere?" But I didn't know which kind of "go away" this was.

I'm also aware that sometimes "Go away" means, "Hey creepy old guy, you're sitting way too close to me in this coffee shop." But that's a different book.

So I just knelt there.

And that's when it began.

My emotions started to swirl, as old and long suppressed hurts rose to the brim of my chest. Paul crying under his bed had become some kind of emotional trigger for me, and what it produced hit me with the force of a tsunami. I was being sucked into an eddy of past feelings that I had tried to bury since my divorce six years earlier.

I strained to pull myself free, but the rush of emotions was too strong. They were coming one after the other, like corpses that had unearthed themselves, each one carrying armfuls of Shame.

I was kneeling there, but was simultaneously

transported back in time to the edge of the Golden Gate Bridge, where I had gone several times during the weeks following Laurie's remarriage and move. And now the wind was swirling around me again, and so was the self-loathing.

I'd been terrified that my boys would grow up to think of me as a stranger. Or worse, to hate me for what I'd done. What else could they feel but disgust once they learned that I had had an affair when they were tiny, that my selfishness had crushed their mother's heart, and that I had betrayed the trust of everyone I cared for? I'd been led to that bridge by the feral imagining that my sons might be better off without me.

That I might be better off without me.

Lost perspective is a cold wet thick fog, and shame is a cancer.

I'd been a young associate pastor in a large church at the time, and our future had been bright. But then I confessed to Laurie, and her heart, along with our lives, was shattered. She took the boys and moved in with her mom, who was awoken almost every night by the sound of her daughter crying in her sleep. She'd slip in to rub Laurie's back, but there was no consolation that could rush her healing, or ebb her tears.

It's been more than twenty-one years since I told her what I'd done, and I can still remember the ache in her voice when she asked how she could ever trust me again.

I had no answer.

When I confessed my affair to the head pastor, he wanted to find a way to restore me. But he didn't know, and I didn't explain, that the crisis of faith that had led up to my choice, and the weeks of living a double life since, had been too much for me. I had nothing left.

Sometimes a man will choose a different kind of pain over the one he lives with, because the change will seem like relief. Such a man is a fool who just hasn't realized it yet.

Everyone had thought they knew me, but no one had. I'd been teaching people to trust God, but wasn't even willing to trust my own wife with the full extent of my OCD. I'd been living a lie, doubting everything I'd always believed, and when I chose self-destruction as my way out, I hurt hundreds of people in the process. Not only had I betrayed someone they loved, I'd broken the trust they'd put in me. Most vilified me and withdrew, and I understood why.

And so my career was over, my severance pay signed willingly over to Laurie, my reputation and future destroyed, and my faith dead. But worst of all, my family was gone.

Silence filled the last prepaid weeks in our apartment. There were no happy sounds of boys playing down the hall, and each night I'd hear "Goodnight Daddy, I love you" over telephone lines, instead of through their bedroom door. When I reached to turn the lights off on another empty day, I'd see their faces on Kodak paper instead of on their pillows.

I had done this to all of us, and it could not be undone.

If hope is a thing with feathers, I had managed to reach into where it was perched and crush its hollow bones.

*   *   *

And when hope is dead, so is meaning and purpose. And then comes the numb blindness that led me to the bridge with the intention to jump during the following weeks.

But there was also a whisper on the wind each time I stood there. It carried the words from a letter I'd received months earlier from a young man in his twenties. He said I had talked to him when he was a teenager thinking about suicide. He wanted to thank me for telling him about the devastation that's left behind in the lives of a family in the wake of suicide. He said that this thought is what had kept him alive.

And then it did the same for me.

Sometimes the hand of God is only visible in retrospect.

*   *   *

The day I moved the few things I had left into storage, a widow named Donna, whose son I had helped a year earlier, saw me in a McDonald's. I'd never met her before, and she came over to me because she could see I was undone. Her own loss made it possible for her to recognize it in others.

She invited me to stay in her guest room, where I lived and rarely got out of bed for five months. Depression had become my tangible enemy, and she never judged me. She just poured kindness on me, until it became clear that I wouldn't heal unless she asked me to leave. As she sat on the edge of the bed and told me why I had to go, her tears were proof that she was doing it in love.

Her wisdom still stands as one of the greatest gifts poured out on my life.

In order to move forward, I buried my shame deeper than the water under that bridge, and tried to start my life over in a new place. I moved to San Francisco, worked as a part-time security guard and lived in a hotel for three months. It was the kind of place where you can rent a room for an hour, and where low class hookers brought their johns. There was one shared bathroom and shower on each floor. They were filthy, but it was all I could afford.

My OCD was off the charts, and my master's degree meant nothing in this new world. I had no ambition or hope, so when the job ended because of the slow holiday season, I was forced to live in my car.

I'd park somewhere at night, until the cops came to tell me to move. Then I'd drive to a different corner or park under a different overpass. I was too ashamed to ask my family for help, and forgot that home was still a place I could have run.

And that was my life for the next six months.

I walked the streets at night, feeling like a zombie. Everything was numb. My eyes were portals through which I viewed movement around me. I felt separate from everything. Detached. Like I was watching an uncompelling movie about someone else's life from the inside. Though I could touch things, they felt distant, and the noises of the city were drowned out by the silence of the god I had always believed in.

It was a hollow kind of aching.

When I couldn't find odd jobs, I'd beg the small Chinese grocers for food. I'd stand there, gaunt and crying real tears, until they'd give me an apple or banana if I promised to never come back. I was grateful for their mercy.

I remember looking at the wild-eyed crazy homeless people who talked to the air and knowing that I was just one frayed emotional fiber away from snapping and becoming like them. Sometimes I wondered if maybe they weren't better off.

A year earlier thousands had sat hushed to listen to my words, but now I was just another soiled life roaming the streets.

The weeks dissolved into each other, and the only thing I had to cling to was the sound of my boys' voices on the next scheduled phone call. They were living with another man by this time, a better man, and each night when I'd pull the blanket over me in my passenger seat, I'd picture him tucking them in and kneeling to say nighttime prayers next to their beds. He had bought them their first puppies, was their soccer coach and would teach them to ride their first two-wheeler, and I was just a trembling loss.

A leftover gym membership gave me a place to bathe, and I eventually found a job as a waiter, which helped me rent an apartment. My self-loathing moved in with me and seemed to gain power each time I left important events out of my story when I met new people.

And then one day someone who had heard me speak years earlier approached me about speaking at a school. They didn't know what had happened in my life, and I didn't tell. I just said no for months. But they persisted, so I eventually accepted.

My shame kept me from real vulnerability that day, and the great irony was that as a result of my secret pain, there was something in my speaking that others could connect with. They told me that I understood them, that I gave them hope. And so word of mouth gave birth to a speaking career. My clients were unaware of my personal story, and I never used it as a part of my material.

A booking agent suggested I change my name. He told me that my given name of Frank might look good on a truck driver's pocket or the back of a bowling shirt, but that it didn't work well on a brochure. So I chose Tyler, leaving my last name intact, and it became a reminder that I had begun a new life.

And yet, as I found out, a new name does little to chase away demons.

*   *   *

But now, here I was, six years later on Paul's floor, and the inevitable was happening. My unattended wounds were bursting.

I was on my hands and knees now so I wouldn't fall.

A sob from beneath the bed pulled me back into the moment, and I was hit by the fact that I was kneeling there in my child's room, next to a bed and on a carpet that was provided by someone else.

A familiar heaviness had settled into my gut.

Things were never meant to be this way. My boys should be growing up in my house, but here my son was crying under a bed that I had never sat on to read him a story, and in a room I rarely got to see. And I had caused all of this.

I was grateful that Laurie's husband loved our boys so well, but the constant hole in my breast was throbbing now, no longer willing to be the hidden backdrop of my life. And like the frog, there was still nothing I could do to make things go back to the way they were intended.

Another sob. This time from my chest.

I knew I had to hold it together for Paul's sake, so I wiped my eyes, and yet I still didn't know what to do. His words echoed inside. "Go away."

Was he right? Should I? Did I even belong here?

But then something compelled me, like a whisper from God, and I knew what I needed to do.

I compressed my body into that 10-inch space, and moved in toward him. I had failed in the past, but this was my son, and I needed to go and be where he was.

I slid up behind him as I worked the bed over me, and attempted to spoon his little body. As I reached out, he shrugged my arm off and scooted a little further away.

Then he said it again.

"Go away!"

The lump caught in my throat.

But I stayed.

He needed me to.

I needed me to.

A moment passed, and although he was still crying, and the space between us was full of questions, I breathed out a whisper.

"Paul, I'm sorry I killed your frog."

And I was sorry for so much more.

The air was still, nothing moved, and then a wonderful thing happened.

He leaned his little back into my chest.

I wrapped my arm around him, he received it, and the rhythm of his crying began to slow. I held him a bit tighter, and said it again.

"Paul, I'm so sorry."

"It's" – sob – "okay Dad" – sob – "I know you didn't mean to" – sob.

His forgiveness washed over me. I received it, and discovered that it had brought something else with it. Something with feathers.

And I knew, for the first time in all the years, that I now needed to begin to forgive myself. Not for the frog, but for all the other things I could never change. I didn't know it yet, but that singular understanding was the beginning of the greatest healing in my life. As I lay there, I felt hope warm me. It was seeping through his back, and into my chest.

*   *   *

We stayed still for a little while, and then we talked about other stuff. Important stuff. We spoke about death, and how we need each other, and eventually we even talked about forgiveness.

I told him that I was learning that when we're sad, we shouldn't try to handle it alone. That it's good to talk about it. To be honest.

I said this more for myself than him.

He said, "I already know that dad."

"You're pretty smart then Buddy."

"Smarter than you?"

"Never!" I poked him, and he laughed.

We were both quiet again for a moment, and it felt comfortable.

Then I told him that his frog was in Heaven. Yup, that's right. Heaven. Oh yes, I fabricated theology right there on the spot, and felt pretty good about it too.

He asked what Heaven was like and I told him that I think it's like chocolate-chip ice cream at midnight, only better.

He asked, "Do you think we can go to Heaven tonight at the hotel?" and laughed again.

We decided it would be good to crawl out, find an empty matchbox, and go have a funeral. With solemn respect we placed the deceased in his coffin, and then Paul said to wait as he disappeared into the house. He came back holding three popsicles, so we could use a couple of the sticks to make a cross. We put the funeral on hold, sat in the sun with Spencer and enjoyed our frozen juice on a stick.

Healing was happening.

While we ate, Spencer suggested that we do the kind thing and crush the other frog too, in order to help it avoid the lonely life it was destined to lead without its dead friend.

My son, Spencer Kevorkian. Mr. Euthanasia. The Dr. of Death.

I thought about how his sweet gift of empathy would be helpful to him in life.

We fixed the sticks together and Paul wrote "Frog" on the cross-member with a Sharpie. The funeral was respectful. Laurie attended, and we all said something nice. Even Spencer spoke, without any jokes, and I was proud of him because it's hard to keep funny under control.

We set the other frog free in the woods, and got in

the car to head off for our weekend together. We waved goodbye to Laurie, and I heard Paul in the backseat say, "What kind of a dad shows up and smushes his little kid's frog?"

The boy has a hard heart.

I threatened to smush him if he didn't straighten up, and Spencer offered to help.

*   *   *

When I drove away after our weekend, I was smiling. Not only because Paul had forgiven me for the frog crushing, but because I could still feel the flutter of wings in my soul.

A few years later, when Laurie and I agreed that they were old enough, I told them about my greatest failures. They forgave me then, as they still do now, living full and happy lives in their twenties.

They've taught me that forgiveness is more powerful than shame, and that it carries redemption in its arms.

And as far as I can tell, Spencer still hasn't assisted in any suicides, frog or otherwise. And that makes me proud.

Out of the Fog

I first saw him on a darkened stretch of sidewalk in San Francisco. It was evening, and colder than January should have been. I was wishing I was in my warm apartment.

The air was crisp, almost brittle, and he stood in silhouette, backlit by a streetlamp. He was leaning against a building with one leg bent, his foot resting on the brick treatment behind him.

The sun had set hours earlier, and the fog was taking its nightly stroll from the bay into the city. It swirled up the street in slow motion, dancing and eddying around doorways and newspaper stands as it came.

As I got closer, I noticed the rhythm of his breath puffing out before his face, and how the few others on the sidewalk steered a wide arc around him as they passed.

I hadn't planned on being out in the cold. I'd been

tricked into it. Before I could think, my pretty friend Mia had suggested that we split up and give sweatshirts away to homeless people.

It's not fair when a girl is pretty. It makes it hard to think sometimes. Like when I should have said, "No! They will still be homeless tomorrow, and now is the time when you should rub my shoulders and feed me grapes as I lean my head upon thy lap."

I knew this was selfish, especially given my background, but I'd been helping her move since 9 a.m., which she'd also tricked me into, and all day I'd been looking forward to that moment when she'd praise me for my strength and generous humility.

Moving is an art, and I had been the artist. I deserved some major adoration.

But before I could figure out how to get out of it and still come across like a good person, she had emptied half a box of sweatshirts into my arms and sent me into the weather.

I didn't want to be out here, and obviously, neither did my nipples. My goal was to give the sweatshirts away as fast as possible so I could get back for some significant me time.

She'd taken her pile in the other direction.

When I noticed him, I only had two sweatshirts left, and was practicing a speech about how important it is to humble ourselves to help the less fortunate, hoping it might get me even more praise once this philanthropic business was over.

I walked up to him with the sweatshirts tucked under my arm and my hands stuffed into my pockets, hoping he wouldn't want to shake.

"Hi," I said, and he lowered the paper cup he was holding.

"I'm giving sweatshirts away and was wondering if you'd like one."

He straightened himself, pushed off the wall, and I couldn't read his face in the dim light. I thought that maybe he was offended by the offer.

"I don't mean to insult you, but would you like one of these?"

I held the blue and red sweatshirt out in front of him.

He tapped his chest and said, "Fa—me?"

I wondered if he'd been drinking.

I nodded.

"Cood I halv that one?" He spoke slowly, and pointed at the U.C. Berkeley hoodie in my right hand. His words were labored as he wrestled against some kind of speech impediment, trying to pin each sound down, one after the other.

His eyes blinked with each success.

As I handed him the blue one, an apartment light

turned on above our heads, and I could see that he was older than I'd thought. He looked maybe forty. His leathered skin showing the years he'd spent on the streets.

"Go ahead, try it on."

He didn't smell like alcohol.

"O – K" he said, putting his cup between his foot and the building. He pulled it over his head and struggled to find one of the armholes. I could hear him giggling from inside as he poked about.

There was a childlike quality to him and I smiled.

Once he had succeeded in getting it on, he looked down and smoothed it against his chest.

"Awe-most got stuck in-dear." He giggled again.

"Eeed looks gwait, huh?"

"Yea, a perfect fit. Go Berkeley!"

I felt silly for saying this, until he said, "Mmmay-be I shood git a job dare as a spee-t-ch tee-ch-er," and laughed out loud.

"Tank-ee-you for be-in so nice-sa ta me."

I pointed back toward Mia's apartment and said, "Actually it's my friend who's nice. I'm just doing her a favor."

"Wool ee-you done me a fay-va too nd I tank-ee you." He looked down and smoothed the sweatshirt again.

"My name's Tyler."

I reached out and we shook hands.

"I'm Toe-nee."

"Hey, are you hungry?" The words were out of my mouth before my brain previewed them.

"There's a McDonald's just down the street. Want anything?"

"Wheely?"

"Sure. I was just headed there." I lied.

"Come on." I motioned him to join me.

He picked up his cup, rolled his hands up under the front of his new sweatshirt and we both leaned into the fog together.

As we walked, I didn't know what to say so I asked if he was having a hard time finding a job. He explained that four years earlier he'd had an accident that had somehow affected his speech and motor skills.

"Eva seence den, no-one'll geeve me a job."

He mentioned that he was still trying, and hoped to get one before he turned thirty, next summer.

I was stunned at how young he was, but tried not to show it. I thought of what a luxury it had been to have a car to sleep in all those months. It had protected me from the cold and drying fingers of the city.

"I wan-na work, n-my spee-t-ch is get-in a liddle bedder, so I wow-nt geev up."

An icy gust pushed against us, slipping its hand down the back of my collar. I shivered.

"Tank-e-you for com-in out in da co-wald Tile-a."

I said I was glad I had and then he asked about me. What I did for a living.

I began to tell him, but then our lives seemed so out of balance that I cut my answer short. I felt embarrassed that people paid me to go around telling stories.

He said he thought I must be good at it, and hoped to hear me do it sometime, and I thought that was a kind thing for him to say.

Then he mentioned that he'd seen me around the neighborhood, and I was embarrassed again. I lived just a couple blocks away and walked these streets almost every day and had never noticed or reached out to him.

To have been spared, and to have forgotten, is an ugly ingratitude.

When we got to McDonald's, he opened the door for me. We walked in and everyone waiting to order stepped as far away from us as they could while still keeping their place in line.

"Tank-e-you for brin-in me in here Tile-a."

I nodded.

I wanted to tell the people to stop looking at him.

When our turn came at the counter I said, "Tony, get whatever you want."

He asked, "Cain I-ee have a beeg coke?"

"Sure, anything."

"Tank-e-you." His eyes were wide as he looked at the menu on the wall and asked if he could have a kid's meal.

I said "Just one?"

By the time we were done, I'd talked him into two kid's meals, an apple pie, a big coke and a chocolate milkshake.

He was very excited about his milkshake.

I paid, then rushed to open the door for him as he concentrated on carrying all his food. He held it like treasure.

He hadn't seemed to notice everyone staring at us, but just before we stepped outside, he turned and said, "Halv a guud nite," and nodded to them with a warm smile.

We stepped out and I said how happy I was that we'd met. Then he did something unexpected. He bent down, put his dinner on the sidewalk, and then put his hand high up on the top of my shoulder so that it partially cupped the back of my neck.

"Ya know Tile-a, I-ya don't want you ta wor-eey-abowt-me, O – K?"

I was caught off guard and didn't have a response. I just nodded.

"Don't wor-eey-abowt-me, O – K?" His tone was gentle, but more emphatic now.

I fumbled. "Um, okay."

The fog moved across our shoulders, and the noises

around us seemed to disappear into its mist.

With his hand still cupping my neck he said, "Ya see Tile-a, da way I see-id-is-dis. As long as der-is people in da world like you – ta take care-au-me – nd as long as der-is people I kin take care-au – da way i see-id-is I-ma gonna be O – K."

He moved his hand off, and motioned me closer.

"Come eer."

I took a half step forward and he moved into me, bending his face into my chest. He hugged me, and I hugged him back.

He patted me and I could hear his voice coming from my chest saying, "Tank-ee-you Tile-a, tank-ee-you."

We let go, and he put his hand on my shoulder again.

"God baless-you Tile-a."

I muttered, "He just did Tony."

I tried to thank him for what he'd said, but my words got stuck. I think he could see that my heart was full, so he nodded, picked up his food, smiled, nodded again, and turned down the sidewalk.

I took my time walking back to Mia's apartment. I needed to let things marinate.

With about a block to go I passed an old woman with a shopping cart piled high with junk, and offered her the red sweatshirt. She snatched it and screamed, "Did you steal this from me? I'll call the police if you don't get away from me!" She said this with such volume and ferocity that I'm sure thousands of male penguins in Antarctica looked up from their huddling and dropped their eggs.

I smiled and backed off as she stuffed the sweatshirt into a grocery bag that was tearing from the pressure, and watched as she wheeled her life down the sidewalk.

She was a happy crazy person. I knew this because she kind of danced away and I could hear her singing my favorite song, *Let's Stay Together*, by Al Green.

This made me happy and I wondered what she'd be like as a girlfriend.

Some people just make a bad first impression.

Eventually I got to Mia's, and when she buzzed me up, I held the door open and looked back down the street through the fog for a moment and wondered if maybe Tony was one of those angels you hear about in church, who come disguised to give us gifts.

I stood a bit longer, took a deep breath of the brisk air and headed up the stairs.

When I walked in her door, Mia must have seen something in my expression because she asked if I was okay. I wasn't ready to talk, so I just said, "Yea, no everything's great."

I went to the sink and while I was washing my hands said, "I think I may have just met my dream woman and soul mate about a block from here."

But Mia had stopped paying attention because of the TV, so she just said, "That's nice."

My shoulders felt tight, both from the move and the cold, so I went over and sat next to her on the couch and said, "How about a backrub?"

"Wow, that'd be great!" she said, as she turned her back toward me and leaned a bit forward. "Not too hard though, I'm kind of sore."

So I began rubbing her shoulders.

Sometimes pretty girls bug me.

Africa

The water beneath our rowboat seemed to absorb all sound as dusk spread silence across the face of the lake. Even the baboons and birds hidden in the lush growth along the banks had quieted their cries.

Perhaps they sensed the coming attack.

The angled light of sunset was gathering reds and oranges from the dust hovering over the distant Serengeti. But there was no dust here. The air hung heavy over the water and felt wet, as though Nature herself were trying to quiet the world.

The surface mirrored what the dropping sun had flung across the west, but my eyes weren't drawn in that direction. Instead, my attention was focused toward the darkening east and to what had just slipped its giant eyes beneath the surface, about forty feet from our boat.

She was angry and she was coming for us.

We knew this because the reverse wake, created by four-tons of displaced water pressing up against the surface from below, was moving fast in our direction. She was motivated by the instinct to protect her baby, and was charging across the bottom of the lake with the intent to kill.

My hands grabbed the rough wood around me, as though this might hold back her attack, and my fear.

On land a hippo can outrun an Olympic athlete, and submerged, they move with the grace of a galloping thoroughbred. At fourteen feet long, and with twenty-inch teeth, they kill more humans in Africa each year than any other animal. Deaths sometimes happen on land, at night while they furrow for food. But most occur as they protect their territory by ramming boats, turning them over and crushing their prey between jaws that can open up to four feet wide.

This was not the Africa of Hollywood; it was the Africa of Dale Hamilton, a forty-five-year-old man as untamed as the world that surrounded us. We were about two hundred yards from the dock, our only connection to the remote and steep banks.

Dale's wife Chris, who sat behind him at the front of our boat, had grown nervous as he had paddled toward this big female. He'd been playing with nature, but now the panic in his eyes told me things were no longer under his control.

She was gaining on us.

As he leaned his weight back into the oars, only his face betrayed his fear. His dipping and pulling was so smooth, that like the charging giant, it made no noise.

Just thirty feet now.

The pain in my lungs alerted me to the fact that I was holding my breath.

Twenty-five feet.

As Chris spoke, her words were quick and sharpened by panic.

"Dale. Faster!"

Phantom spiders began crawling over the skin on my back and neck.

Twenty feet.

The surface showed that she had sped up. I tried not to cry out as my heart thundered in my ears.

Fifteen feet.

The weight of the air seemed to conspire with the beast, pressing down as if to slow our escape.

Twelve feet.

The boat felt small. Thin. Even frail.

Ten feet.

Chris spoke again. Just a word uttered in a terrified whisper.

"Dale."

His name, her hope.

He kept pulling.

Eight feet.

"Dale." Louder this time.

Five feet.

The giant began to rise. I could see her now through the murky water. She was an aberration. The outline of her ghostly form bulging and flowing with the distorted tricks of dim and bent light. Her huge head came into focus first, just a couple of feet below and coming up fast. I leaned back and my panic broke the surface at the same time she did. She was as big as a minivan, and moved enough water to rock us from back to front.

She snorted a plume five-feet into the air and let out a grunt so loud it rattled the oars. She opened her mouth an impossible distance and the waning light allowed me to see past her teeth and deep into her throat. I fell backwards, off my plank seat, and landed on the bottom of the boat between Dale's knees, hitting my head on an oar as I pulled my feet into myself.

She snapped her mouth shut, grunted again, and stopped her pursuit.

Her eyes were at least two feet apart, and their horizontal pupils stared at me as I sat there feeling trivial.

She'd sent a message, and it was personal. None of us were anything to her. She didn't care about me, my plans, dreams, or loves. I was nothing more than an annoyance that she would as soon crush as chase away.

I felt small. Breakable. Expendable in the large scheme of things.

And I was right.

All the air had left my body.

I was still shaking as I climbed past Dale to the front of the boat. Chris slid over to welcome me.

As the gap widened, we were silent and aware that the hippo could have had us if she'd wanted. And yet for some reason she'd decided not to break the shell of our bodies, causing life to leave us through the cracks.

She kept watching from her new post.

Dale slowed the boat and we began to coast. The only sound now was the dripping from his upheld oars. I could feel the eyes of all the animals hidden in branches that had ceased their motion to watch what was going on.

We were not the apex hunters here.

The silence that hung around us exploded as Dale let out a laugh so loud that it bounced back at us from the edge of the shore. The startle almost sent me falling into the dark water.

His head was rocked back, and he slapped the paddles on the surface in delight. He hooted as though we'd just climbed off a thrilling roller coaster that was built according to strict safety standards.

He looked back at us and said, "Let's do it again!"

"It's not funny Dale!" This time Chris's tone had a severe edge and she said his name for emphasis.

But then, as she turned and looked away toward the west, where the blanket of darkness was being pulled up to the chin of the world, I saw her smile to herself as though she was remembering that it was this same crazy passion for life, and the pushing against its boundaries, that had caused her to fall for Dale in the first place. This world of theirs was full of peril and risk, and she knew he needed to play in it, not to test its limits, but to reassure himself of his own.

Africa was his life. He moved to its rhythm. And in her smile I could see that she loved him for it. She turned again, and I watched her watch him while he paddled us in, telling stories over his shoulder all the way.

He seemed bigger than life. Almost fictional.

*   *   *

As we climbed onto the dock my legs were still weak, and endorphins were dancing through my veins.

Dale looked at me and smiled.

"Your hands are shaking. You sure you don't want to do it again?"

"No thanks." I laughed. "When my dad suggested I

get together with you guys for dinner, I didn't expect that you'd feed me to a hippo."

"She was beautiful. Did you see those eyes?"

"I think she winked at me."

"You should send flowers."

My parents, who had spent most of their lives in Africa, had known Dale and Chris for years and had arranged our meeting. I was born in Zambia, and lived there until we moved to the States when I was seven. As a result, I'd always felt drawn back to the continent, and had visited many times. When I learned that they'd be vacationing nearby, we agreed to meet for dinner. They felt like old friends before dessert was served.

Dale tied up the boat and they both walked me up to my lodge. On the way I turned to Chris and said, "You're a nurse. Can't you slip something into his food to make him more sane?"

She smiled and as Dale shouldered me I said, "I'm not messing with you Dale. All during dinner I felt like I'd seen you before, but couldn't place it. I just figured it out. You were great in Bloodsport."

He laughed, "Okay, first of all Chuck Norris wasn't in Bloodsport, that was Jean-Claude Van Damme. And second, I'm way better looking than Chuck Norris could ever dream of being."

I laughed and he rubbed his beard.

He went on, "Almost every day somebody tells me that. Chuck Norris is huge here. The Africans love him. That's how I was able to borrow that rowboat. I just go with it."

We had reached my door so I turned to them, "I've got to get up early for my safari, but thanks for spending the evening with me. And Chris, thanks for not letting me die out there."

Dale laughed, "Maybe next time."

I said, "You're not normal."

"I know, but that's why people love me." His eyes betrayed his pretend pride.

Then he turned sincere, "Don't forget what we told you about the cool little island on the other side of Lake Victoria where we live. If you ever want to see the real Africa, you've got a place to stay. Remember, it's called 'Bumbire Island'. No matter how many years from now, okay. You've got an open invitation."

I nodded and said, "And I live on a really cool island too. So if you ever want to see the real Hawaii, contact me and I'll give you the name of a great hotel on Maui."

"But I thought you lived on Kauai."

"I do."

We laughed, hugged goodbye and then Dale put his heavy hand on my shoulder, "I meant what I said. Anytime you want to come, just let us know. We'd love it."

I believed him and went to bed that night unaware

that an important decision in my future would bring me to Bumbire, looking for perspective.

*   *   *

It was three years later, and a late summer afternoon when I first saw the island. My body was feeling the affects of the thirty-hour commute from the West. The final leg had been over rough waters in a small boat, but I knew this was where I needed to be.

Bumbire was long and narrow, had dense jungle near the water, and some clearings as the hills rose. The banks were steep, and as we approached the dock I could see the hint of one rugged house, tucked into the bush about thirty feet from the shoreline. There were no roads, telephone poles or power lines. This was raw and untouched Africa.

To get here, Amali, my African boat driver, had taken us past many other undeveloped islands. Lake Victoria is more than 26,000 square miles, so our trip had taken hours.

As we talked, he was fascinated to hear about the clear oceans of Hawaii, and said he'd spent his entire life on water because his dad used to hunt crocodiles when he was small.

Naturally I mentioned that I often caught geckos with

my bare hands.

He seemed impressed.

As he docked the boat he said he was Dale's friend, that everyone in Tanzania was Dale's friend, so he'd come up and say hi.

I stepped out onto the dock with my backpack in one hand, and turned to make sure I hadn't left anything in the boat. Just then, deep throaty barks coming from the other end of the dock caught my attention.

I turned to see Dale's 135-pound rottweiler running down the dusty path at the far end of the dock. I stiffened a bit and Amali laughed.

"No need to be afraid, he wouldn't hurt a butterfly."

The dogs fur gleamed black, and the tan markings on his cheeks, muzzle and eyebrows made him appear to be smiling. His undocked tail was wagging.

Chuck Norris was in the distance, limping and waving as he came.

I waved back, and asked Amali if the limp was from the floatplane crash I'd heard about.

"Nope. Motorcycle accident. He should have died. His bone came through his leg and he was bleeding into the dirt. He somehow managed to drag himself a half mile to get help."

The dog reached the far end of the dock, and something caught his attention. He stopped and the tone of his barking changed. He began moving his large head up and down, jumping forward, then back, as he hopped around something at his feet.

Amali saw it before I did. A snake had slithered from the rocks beneath, and up onto the dock near the shore.

He grabbed my arm and moved toward the boat, but I shrugged him off. I knew that Africans were notoriously afraid of snakes, and he'd obviously forgotten about the geckos.

As he scampered back into the boat he said, "Come please," and reached for the rope. I turned to him and said, "No worries, I watch Animal Planet."

Then he said, "King Cobra. Come now." And I froze.

Dale was already running, and he yelled, "No Duke!"

The cobra was about eight feet long, and with a third of its body now raised up from the ground, its huge head was eye level with the dog. Its hood was spread, and it let out a bone chilling sound that was more growl than hiss.

The dog kept circling, barking.

Still erect and fiercely aggressive, the snake moved forward.

"Back Duke. No!"

But it was too late.

Both the barking and hissing stopped as the snake spit venom in Duke's eyes and struck his thick muzzle. The huge dog let out a yelp, took three steps toward Dale and fell over dead.

My backpack dropped at my side.

Dale went after the snake with vengeance, using the machete that hung from his belt.

I watched in horror.

When he was done he had killed the cobra more than once and the air was full of dust. He left it laying there in pieces and went over to the body of his dog. He sat down beside it, rubbing Duke's ears and shoulders and back.

"You're a good boy Duke. Good boy."

But Duke was gone.

Nothing moved except the water lapping the pilings at the base of the dock.

I was stunned.

After a moment, Dale stood, wiped his face, and came toward me. He hugged me and said, "Karibu. Welcome to Africa."

I said, "Dale, I'm so sorry."

He said, "It's hard. I loved that dog. We see lots of death here."

So much death, it seemed, that the living had to learn to grieve it quickly.

"Let's get you settled and then you can help me bury my dog."

He bent and picked up my backpack and said, "The Africans say that the only good snake is a dead snake. But if you're bitten, don't try to kill it. Just get to us as fast as you can and remember the order and color of its stripes. This way we'll know what kind of antivenom to give you."

I was still shaken by what I'd just seen and told him the snake stripe thing was a problem since I'm colorblind. He smiled, hit me on the shoulder with his open hand and said, "You'll probably be okay! Let's head up to the house, Chris is excited to see you."

Probably?

I felt like I was in a remake of Indiana Jones.

He threw my backpack over his shoulder, put his arm around Amali, and as we began to walk, looked down at him and said, "Karibu."

Amali smiled, "Karibu Bwana." Then, pulling him closer, Dale looked at me and said, "Amali's got seven daughters, and is still trying for a son," and laughed.

Amali giggled.

They spoke in Swahili for a moment and then Dale turned to me again, "You're going to love the place we've fixed up for you."

"Great. Thanks." I still couldn't believe what I'd just seen.

As we walked past, I tried not to look at Duke.

"You'll be sleeping up in the clinic. We're not done building it yet, but the roof's on. There's no windows or door, but it's on top of the hill and has a great view. It's just up that trail there." He pointed at a narrow opening through the thick jungle brush to the right.

"We'll give you a flashlight because that trail is what the hippos use to get food." Both he and Amali smiled as if he'd just said, "Your suite is next to the pool, and room service is available till midnight."

Still smiling he said, "You look worried. Don't be. We'll keep you safe."

I missed my geckos.

*   *   *

The next morning, I decided that the only thing worse than waking to a spider that is the size of my hand, has hair on its legs, eyes as big as a Chihuahua's, and lifts its body a full inch off the surface as it moves – is to see that same spider from underneath looking up at it's underbelly just inches from my face as I open my eyes for the first time and focus on the mosquito net just above my head.

I almost wet myself.

This was freaking Jurassic Park!

I didn't know what to do.

I swear, at that precise moment the spider lifted a leg, bent its head, looked down at me with one of its eight eyes and licked its lips.

I'm not normally afraid of spiders, but ones that can

eat my head tend to give me the willies. So I hit it from beneath with my hippo-spotting flashlight, and it actually made a thud when it hit the floor. It looked back over its shoulder as if to say, "Is that all you got?" then flipped me off and sauntered out the door like it was headed to the fields to throw a football with its buddies.

I wanted Starbucks.

I decided to name the spider Hannibal, because I was sure he'd be back that night with a nice bottle of Chianti tucked under one arm.

Ten minutes later, as I walked down the jungle path to Chris and Dale's house, the breeze alerted me to the fact that the hairs on my neck were still standing on end.

The pathway had changed overnight. The overhead vines had grown so much that I had to duck most of the way. I carried a stick, which I swiped in front of my face to push aside the spider webs that had been spun after dark. They were covered in dew and beautiful, but all I could think about was my fear of meeting Hannibal's father out here somewhere.

I opened the kitchen door and was greeted by the smell of bacon, toast and eggs. Dale was at the stove and said, "Morning! I'm making a fancy breakfast. Sleep well?"

I said that I had, and as I set the table, told him about the spider.

He said, "Maybe tonight he'll bring some scissors to

cut the net," and belly laughed.

I mumbled, "And maybe today I'll bring Jean-Claude Van Damme to kick your ass."

He laughed again, called me Clarice and said, "This talk is making me hungry. Sit. Let's eat."

Chris had come in and moved the plate of food to the table. "You're going to gain weight this summer. Dale cooks like a fat grandma from the south."

As we ate I thanked them for listening the night before, while we'd sat around their fire pit. They'd asked about my sons, who were now ten and twelve, and the emotion had caught in my throat. In all the years it had been the first time I'd found the strength to verbalize how much I missed my boys.

There are some sorrows so deep, that to stir their surface is to risk drowning.

They listened in the firelight as I explained that back when Laurie had moved, I'd wanted to relocate to be closer, but she'd said her husband's job would force them to a different state every three years. That had changed now, and so I was trying to figure out what to do.

"I just don't want to miss out on anymore of their lives."

Dale said, "I don't blame you."

I nodded and explained that a few weeks earlier, Laurie had begged me not to move. She was afraid it would be too disruptive. The boys were doing great and she said my regular visits were perfect for them. I'd always trusted her wisdom, and couldn't argue with how great they were doing, but still didn't know what to do.

And now, sitting next to me at the breakfast table, Chris reached out and rubbed my arm for a moment and said, "I'm glad you told us."

Dale stretched for more eggs. "I woke in the night and couldn't get back to sleep, thinking about all the stuff you've been through. I was trying to figure out what I'd do if I were you."

These two hardly knew me and were already carrying my weight on their shoulders.

Dale continued. "There's a place we're going to take you today that I hope will help somehow. We've got some friends who live about a half-hour boat ride from here. You'll see when we get there. It may be my favorite place on earth."

Chris smiled.

*   *   *

As we climbed into the boat Chris said, "Try not to touch the water. It's infested with a microscopic worm called bilharzias."

I stared down at the surface.

"It's a parasite that gets into your body through your skin and lays eggs in your digestive tract. If it's not treated it causes liver failure, and death."

"And you guys live here, why?"

Dale smiled and called me a sissy.

And he was right.

The wind had picked up so the boat ride was rough.

As we passed one of the larger islands, I noticed a somber expression come across Dale's face. When I asked about it, he said that there were about a thousand boys between 18 and 21 who lived there.

"They come because they can make twice the money fishing for Nile perch for the big companies. They get two dollars a day."

He nodded toward the island and said, "Lots of them are my friends, and eighty percent are HIV positive and will be dead in three to five years. They get it from the female cooks who double as prostitutes."

Death is everywhere in Africa.

As we continued past, Dale and Chris watched the island and there was heaviness in their expression.

*　　*　　*

When we climbed out of the boat I thought, "This is his favorite place?"

The microclimate here was different than Bumbire. The ground was a dry and compressed brown dirt. There was little natural growth except some skeletized bushes scattered around.

About sixty yards from the water were two buildings that looked like rundown dormitories from the Civil War era. They were facing each other with a huge baobab tree between them. The only redeemable thing about the place was some grass that blanketed the ground beneath the tree. The shade and green looked soft and inviting.

We walked toward it and Dale said, "There're some people I want you to meet. They don't know we're coming."

As we walked onto the grass, some small children spotted us and came running from the building to our right, shouting "Bwana, Bwana." "Mister, Mister."

Dale ran for them. When he reached the first little girl, he grabbed her and sat down as the others piled on top, all giggles, kisses and laughter. There were about twenty of them, all under four-years-old.

This orphanage was their home.

It was then that I noticed a little boy and girl standing back and holding hands as they watched from a distance.

Dale was on his back now, little ones buzzing around, all taking turns jumping on his stomach. Doctors had told him years ago that he must leave Africa, because if he got malaria one more time it would likely kill him. But here he was, stubborn, strong and tickling children.

Perhaps his proximity to death had something to do with his tenderness.

As I watched, I understood that his favorite place wasn't a place. It was these kids.

Once the tickle-fest was over, Dale introduced me to all the little ones staring up with wide brown eyes. He told them to call me "Mwanamke Tyler." I found out later it was Swahili for "Lady Tyler." They all giggled, some of them covering their mouths and bent at the waist.

It was a beautiful sound.

Then Dale asked about the two who had hung back when we arrived, and we learned that Enzi and his smaller sister, Johari, had shown up at midnight the evening before.

They had been alone in the dark when Dale's friend heard the knock and opened the orphanage door. When he asked what he could do for them, the four-year-old boy had looked down at his two-year-old sister, whose hand he was holding, and said, "Kwa sababu wapi tutaqwenda?" "Where else can we go?"

Thrust too soon into being a man, his small voice was her only hope.

Their dad had died before Johari was born, and their mom had died a couple of weeks later during childbirth. Just yesterday, the uncle who had taken them in, sent them away because his own wife was now dead and he couldn't care for them any more.

AIDS has always found a way to reach its fingers beyond the bodies it infects, and into the lives of those who are dependent on the sick one. These secondary victims are most often children.

Sent out alone, Enzi and Johari's combined weight couldn't have been more than forty pounds. They had slept in the same bed last night because they had refused to let go of each other's hand.

When we heard this, Dale went to them, got down on his good knee and began to talk and make them laugh. Then after a few minutes, had them involved in the games of their new brothers and sisters. Their giggles reminded me of my own sons when they were small. If it weren't for the lucky matter of longitude and latitude at their birth, I realized, my boys might have ended up somewhere like this.

As they played, the tentativeness that comes from great loss wasn't yet gone from Enzi's or Johari's movements. When they breathed, their intake of air still stuttered across their throats, reminiscent of all the crying that had already past, and was still yet to come.

But they were home now.

*   *   *

After the kids ate and went to bed, we all sat around a campfire about fifty yards from the buildings. We ate barbequed goat with our hands, and threw the bones over our shoulders into the brush.

The others went in to check on the children, leaving Dale and me alone.

"Do you hear that?" he asked as he looked back over his shoulder into the dark.

I listened. Nothing but crickets.

"No baboon sounds. It means something spooked them."

More silence.

I said, "Thanks for letting me be here this summer."

"Of course. It's going to be fun."

"I feel a bit embarrassed about last night, sitting there by the fire, tearing up and going on about my pain."

"Why should that embarrass you?"

"Well, after all I've seen today, it makes my pain seem kind of small."

He poked at the fire with a stick and said, "No one's pain is small."

I thought for a moment and said, "Sometimes I feel overwhelmed."

He said, "Yea, you've lost a lot."

There was more silence, then he spoke again.

"It's quiet here, just you and me around this fire. It

always strikes me in moments like this that there are almost seven billion people out there, all with their own story, making noise somewhere."

"That's a lot of stories."

"It's humbling to think that in about a hundred years, there'll be all new people."

The fire spit an ember as if to punctuate his thought.

He continued. "Before I moved here, I spent a lot of energy trying to control stuff. My life. My circumstances. The people near me. But being around so much death has taught me that there's not much I can control."

He tossed his stick into the flames, reached for another and said, "I couldn't control that hippo when we first met. Or the cobra yesterday, or even Duke. My motorcycle, my plane, even the mosquitoes that keep giving me malaria are out of my control. Heck, a lot of times I can't even control myself, just ask Chris."

He smiled in the firelight and went on, "Like your pain. It's real, but you can't change what's happened anymore than the little kids sleeping over there can make their moms and dads come back to life."

I knew he was right about the past, and asked "So what do you think I should do?"

He said, "I can't tell you if you should move or not. But I can say that the only thing I've found that makes any sense is to try to live based on what's most loving for other people."

I thought of him playing with Enzi and Johari.

He said, "I'm sorry. I'm rambling. Does any of that make sense?"

"Oh, I haven't been listening to a word you've said."

He mumbled, "I'm going to feed you to a hippo tonight."

I said, "In a hundred years, all new hippos."

We laughed.

I continued, "If I don't move, I'll miss out on so much of their lives."

And though neither of us knew it yet, his next words would stick with me, and later guide me to make the hard choice not to relocate to live near my sons.

"It's a tough one," he said. "Knowing what's best is what makes relationships so hard. And we're bound to make tons of mistakes."

He looked at me, "I can't pretend to know what you should do, but maybe Laurie's right. What's best for you might not be what's best for them."

He looked back into the fire and I let his words settle.

"Thanks for talking to me about this."

"You don't have to thank me. It's good for me to think about this stuff too."

"Well, I can't tell you how much it means."

He moved his red-hot stick towards my leg and said,

"You should stop talking, you're starting to sound like a sissy again."

So I spit into the fire to show him how tough I was.

"Nice one," he said.

"Thank you." I sniffed and spit again, but it sort of just sprayed out and we both laughed.

In the silence that followed, he began to rub his sore knee.

I asked, "Living here, how do you know about Hannibal and Clarice?"

"*Silence of the Lambs* was playing on the TV when I was in the hospital one time."

"Hospitals are nice that way."

"Yes they are."

He pointed to the place where his bone had come through the skin and said, "To quote Hannibal Lecter, 'Our scars have the power to show us that our past is real.'"

"Hannibal said that?"

"Yup."

"Who'd have thought?"

"My scars remind me that I'm pretty frail, and maybe that's a good thing."

There was a long pause and the fire hypnotized me.

"When you think about your boys, remember Enzi and Johari. With enough love, even they'll be okay. Kids are resilient, and sometimes the best we can do is to just fumble around and hope to choose the most loving thing. At least then, even if we get it wrong, we know we've done it for the right reasons."

The thought brought me peace.

"Well then," I asked, "I have another question. Is that path I have to walk up every night really a hippo trail?"

"Yup."

"I hate you, you know that right?"

"Yeah, but seven billion people means some of us are expendable."

"You should work in the hospitality industry."

He hit me on the leg and said, "Let's get back, I imagine your spider will be looking for you."

As we walked he said, "There's an old Swahili saying, 'Mwanza nguma.' It means 'The begi..ning is difficult.'" He put his hand on my shoulder and said, "Your boys are going to be okay, and you'll get through this too. We'll help."

And he was right.

*   *   *

After I switched off my flashlight that night, I lay there listening to the sounds of Africa through the open window. It took some time to fall asleep, as the weight of the day, and the faces of all of those children, pressed down on me.

At one point I sat up and looked through my mosquito net and out the window. There were hundreds of lights dotting the lake and spread out toward the west. They came from the boys' fishing boats.

It was beautiful.

Then I remembered that in just three to five years there would be almost all new boys down there. The thought caught in my chest.

I laid back and the faces of Enzi and his little sister slipped into my mind. I knew they were in bed together across that water, and hoped they weren't awake.

Either way, I knew they were still holding hands.

I rolled onto my side, and as my own breath stuttered across my throat I thought, "The beginning is difficult," and drifted off to sleep.

At about 1 a.m. I was woken by a noise behind me on the floor that I couldn't identify. I didn't move, but opened my eyes to blackness. A prickling flowed over my skin.

The sound was intermittent, so I had to wait about ten seconds between each occurrence. I tried to quiet my breathing. When I heard it again it sounded like metal being dragged against the cement floor.

Very slowly I positioned my shaking hand on my flashlight, so that my finger was on the switch.

I waited till it happened again and spun around as I hit the button and the room filled with light.

And there in the middle of the floor was a pair of scissors. As I strained for details through the net, I saw a string tied to them, with the other end laced around the leg of my bed and then back out through the door.

I yelled, "I still hate you!" and heard the sound of Dale giggling as his footsteps disappeared into the night.

We'd love to know what you think about this book.

Please drop us a note at:

BirthdaySuit@me.com

For more information about the author, please go to BSWisdom.com

I owe a great debt to Spencer Bement, who spent hundreds of hours poring over each syllable of this manuscript with me, in an attempt to teach a speaker how to tell stories in written form. Writing is a different art than speaking, just as painting is different than singing. And though I still have much to learn, he has given me the tools to grow.

Thank you Spencer, for the patience you offered as I attempted to make these stories come to life.

Your name deserves to be on the cover of this book as much as mine. I didn't put it there though, because I don't want you suing me for rights later in life. I hope these words are more valuable to you than any amount of money. No seriously, I really hope they are.

Thank You

Thank you Spencer and Paul, for loving me as you have grown into men, for continuing to invite me to be a part of your stories, and just for being so darn fun. I am proud to be your dad.

To Kristen, my heart, for making my story complete, for carrying the weight of my OCD on your back, and for believing that my stories are worth telling. You are home to me and will be my wife.

To Mom and Dad for teaching me that funny is good, and that words are beautiful. And to Barry, Jeanette and Daryl for loving your little brother even though I'm not normal.

To Donna Dunwoody, for taking me in when I was young, broken, and stained. For loving me enough to feed me, and then making me leave when it was time.

To Frank Tate, for helping me turn a clumsy idea into this book, and then helping me get it to the masses. Your genius and friendship are a gift. To Dan Russell, for sitting on a lanai in Maui with me, and convincing me to write a book. To Dighton Spooner for being so generous with your wisdom, friendship, and braised beef short ribs. And to Dave Schenderlein, my friend since 1984, for being honest once again, and right when you said that my first draft was too mushy.

To David Letterman for making me laugh five nights a week since 1983, and for teaching me the power of self-deprecation.

To Stephen King for explaining that I must be willing to murder my darlings, and to David Sedaris and John Steinbeck for proving that storytelling is art.

To David Hahn at Media Connect, for believing in me, and assembling the talent of Alexandra Kirsch, Emily Mullen, Jaime Weinberg and Nina Boutsikaris to handle my PR. I thank each of you for bringing this book to the world. And to Trisha Thompson at Small Batch Books for teaching me that less is more. And to Devin Dailey for the cover, and Todd Ford for making it all look like a book.

A special thank you to everyone who allowed me to use their stories, but especially Laurie. Our boys have an amazing mom, and you are a remarkable friend.

And most of all, thank you God, for the wastefulness of your grace. My life is saturated with it.

CPSIA information can be obtained at www.ICGtesting.com
Printed in the USA
LVOW12s2047131013

356694LV00001B/1/P